THEOLOGY
OF THE CHRISTIAN WORD

THEOLOGY
OF THE CHRISTIAN WORD:
A STUDY IN HISTORY

FREDERICK E. CROWE, S.J.

PAULIST PRESS
New York, N.Y./Ramsey, N.J./Toronto

Copyright ©1978 by
The Missionary Society
of St. Paul the Apostle
in the State of New York

Library of Congress
Catalog Card Number: 78-51595

ISBN: 0-8091-2106-9

Published by Paulist Press
Editorial Office: 1865 Broadway, New York, N.Y. 10023
Business Office: 545 Island Road, Ramsey, N.J. 07446

Printed and bound in the
United States of America

CONTENTS

Introduction 1

1. The Christian Message Begins 7

2. The Christian Message as
   the Word of God 22

3. The Word of God as Truth 43

4. Truth as Grounded in Sources:
   the Quest of *Loci* 58

5. The Sources as Word
   Across Space and Time 80

6. The Primary Word:
   Jesus Christ Yesterday and Today 104

7. The Inner Word of the Spirit .124

Conclusion and Projections 144

Appendix 150

Notes 158

INTRODUCTION

The simplest way to state the purpose of this book is to call it an attempt to organize the history of reflection on the Christian word of God.

The phrase "Christian word of God" is nowhere defined in these pages, and the omission is deliberate; the purpose is not to analyze a reality, but to write a history of a concept, and the history will show that over the centuries there has been no one definition or way of conceiving the "word" in the Christian community; rather, there has been a series of approaches, with one leading to another, and the whole series perhaps pointing only at some future date to a more systematic conception. Indeed, in the beginning the very term itself had to come into use and receive the specific meaning intended at that time; and this forward step was a condition of all subsequent efforts to understand the reality now domiciled in the church. For the present, then, we use the phrase simply to denote that concrete reality of which Saint Luke so frequently speaks in the Acts of the Apostles, as when he writes that the Twelve delegated certain administrative tasks so that they might devote themselves "to prayer and to the ministry of the Word" (6:4).[1]

The history of reflection on this concrete reality looks back to the earliest post-Easter time when it was not even thought of as the word of God, but was simply the message of good news, if indeed it had a name at all at that time. From this beginning it moves forward through various stages that it is the purpose of the book to delineate. First, the message became known as the word of God; then, the word was discovered to have a truth-content that could be concentrated in doctrines; third, there emerged a need to prove those doctrines from the original sources; fourth, the difference between original sources and present doctrines came to light and was explained by a theory of development; fifth, the very possibility of development was grounded in a new conception of the primary word, understood

1

now as God's very activity in creation and the ongoing course of events; and so, finally, we arrive at our day and the reflection now in progress, when the question is how the primary word is still a word of God for us, despite the changes in form and content it has undergone with the passing centuries. Six transitions, and so seven stages, giving us the seven chapters of this book.

The order is naturally chronological, though with a difference to be explained presently. That is, there is a centering on different aspects of the word in ongoing history. The focus is only more or less sharp for different aspects, and certainly never as sharp as we from our vantage point in time are able to make it. Thus when we study the first transition, that from the message to the message as word of God, we center on Saint Luke's writings; for the transition to the truth to be found in the word, we center on the early conciliar period; similarly, we center on Reformation times for the concern to prove the truth from its sources, on Newman's century for the emergence of the notion of development, and on recent times for the last two stages of reflection: the original richness of a word that is God's own deed, and the power of the Spirit that gives permanence to the word through the changes that human historicity renders inevitable.

I have said that there was never as sharp a focus as this in actually occurring reflection, but there was the emergence of a category, or there was an emphasis, or a thematizing, or a specific questioning, or a concentrated concern that allows us to speak of a "focusing" if not of a focus, and this effort to bring a question or an idea to formulation was rewarded at certain periods with an increment of clarity sufficiently notable to give us our stages of history. We have to remember, however, that achieving a certain focus does not deny, but rather supposes, the existence a good deal earlier of the reality, and perhaps even of a rudimentary notion of what was later formulated. Thus, Saint Paul already refers to the message as "the word of God," though it is only with Saint Luke that this becomes a central category; again, there was a concern with truth from the earliest times we can study, though this became a more distinctly conceived and independently operative theme only with the councils; and so on. The chronological sequence, therefore, is not the simple mechanical succession with which one year follows another.

Furthermore, to come to the main point, the operative factor is never simply the passage of time; rather, it is the series of questions arising out of Christian experience and reflection: The sequence is one of ideas ordered genetically and not just temporally. That is, there is generated, through the questioning mind of the believer, a series of approaches to the word of God, with a dependence of later questions on former ones: It is *because of* the focus on truth that we demand the grounds for what is claimed as true; it is *because of* the difficulty of proving a present doctrine from ancient sources that we advert to the difference between past and present and construct a theory of development; it is *because of* the inadequacy of development viewed as a mere explicitation of the implicit that we are forced to study again the real potentiality of a past word, and the real resources we have in the present for hearing that word.

May I emphasize, then, that the purpose in these seven chapters is not scholarship or erudition, but a reflective ordering of the results of such scholarship; that the chief contribution here is to organize a set of ideas, where, however, the organization is not systematic but genetic, and the ideas are not theoretical but historical. That is, there is no *theory* of the word of God set forth in a system that unfolds from some fundamental conception toward the more particular; the unfolding follows rather the opposite direction from particular concrete forms toward more fundamental conceptions. With the help of a succession of interrelated questions to give direction, movement, and structure, I have traced a path through history that reduces the infinite multiplicity of historical detail to a manageable pattern and enables us to locate diverse authors and ideas in relation to one another in a developing sequence. To change the metaphor a bit, the effort is very much to see the forest and not just the trees, to see the forest as a structured pattern and not just as a vague whole, to see the pattern as developing through the dependence of later questions on earlier and not just as a static framework given from the beginning.

There will surely be no objection to the notion of a path through history, or even to calling it an organization of history when this is understood as the discovery of an intelligible sequence; it does suppose a certain selectivity, but every historian necessarily selects data according to some ruling principle, for otherwise there is simply an infinite multiplicity and the world itself would not contain the books needed to record it. But there may well be objection to the particular path I have chosen: Is it too neat? does it do some violence to the data? is it true to the data but too trivial to organize the significant phases of history? I will not try to anticipate the verdict of readers on such questions, except by laboring in the book itself to establish my thesis. But under one heading it does seem desirable to eliminate misconceptions in advance; let me say a word, then, on what *not* to expect in the book.

It is not a work of research in the ordinary sense, for most of the data I use have been searched out and assembled by others, and I simply borrow their results; there is a recurring exception to this rule, in my efforts to study what Christian writers *do* as contrasted with the objective content of what they expressly *conceive* and say,[2] but, again, readers must judge the efficacy of this procedure. Further, it is not a survey of literature on the topic; the literature I use is selected for its relevance to the discovery and mapping of the *transitions* of history, and then only enough is selected to provide a representative picture. It is not a work of biblical theology, or of patristic or medieval or reformation or modern theology; all these pertain to specialist areas, and my purpose is very precisely not to enter those areas in detail, but once more to borrow results from others and link them in an intelligible sequence and pattern. Again, to make sure the obvious is noted, may I say that this is not a history of the religious expansion and vicissitudes of the word in its ontic reality; for example, it does not narrate what Saint Paul called "the swift and glorious course" of the word in some of his churches (2 Thess. 3:1); rather, it is a history of reflection, a study in the history of ideas in one small area.

A final clarification: In this work I have tried to follow the division of tasks set forth in Bernard Lonergan's theological method.[3] In that conception tasks are divided, not primarily according to a *field* or according to *concepts* (roughly material and formal objects), but according to *functions* in a set of eight functional specialties. Thus, "research is concerned to make the data available. Interpretation to determine their meaning. History to proceed from meaning to what was going forward. Dialectic to go

to the roots of conflicting histories, interpretations, researches"
(p. 349); and four further specialties follow in the phase of committed theology. My study is confined then to "what was going
forward,"[4] and that in the limited field of the notion of the word;
it does not (with the exception noted) assemble its own data, or
determine their meaning; much less does it go to the roots of
conflicting ideas, or proceed to the author's own position on the
word of God, with expansion into foundations, doctrines, sys-
tematics, and communications. Historians who are accustomed,
sometimes with great erudition, to perform for themselves the
tasks of research and interpretation may not recognize here the
kind of history they are willing to honor with that name; others
may feel that a history that stops short of evaluation and taking a
stand or deriving lessons for the present is a very truncated
form. But debate on those questions belongs rather to the long
discussion, hardly yet begun, on the merits of Lonergan's great
work. While the debate goes on, there is room also for modest
efforts at implementation such as this.[5] It is perhaps only in a
dialectic between direct critiques and attempted implementation
that we can come to the judgment on *Method* that many feel
must be postponed to the future.

What should not be postponed, however, is grateful ac-
knowledgement of the comments, critiques, and suggestions that
have contributed to this volume. I am indebted especially to
faculty members of Regis College who attended a seminar in
which I first sketched my idea, and to several colleagues who
read my typescript at one stage or another and submitted their
views to me: Robert Croken, Daniel Donovan, Jean-Marc
Laporte, Roderick MacKenzie, Philip McShane, Colin Maloney,
Ben Meyer, Ovey Mohammed, Conn O'Donovan, Brian Peck-
ham, and Edward Yarnold; also to students in the Toronto
School of Theology who in various ways promoted the project. I
am grateful to these persons for the corrections they have made,
for the way they forced me to clarify my purpose and plan, and
for their positive suggestions on the exploration of further pertinent questions. But I express the hope that they will not be too
disappointed that I carried out so few of the latter. I suspect that
they attribute to me an energy and a competence I do not possess; in any case I have had to settle, in regard to many suggestions, with simply defining more clearly the limits of my study.

CHAPTER ONE

THE CHRISTIAN MESSAGE BEGINS

This chapter, which assumes as its task the study of the origins of the Christian word, proceeds in two phases. It will describe the situation in which that word originally presents itself for study by the historian; and it will describe the first stage of history, the form of the word that was destined to be the antecedent of historical movement. A general picture of the original situation can be gained through a rough inventory of elements pertaining to the word, set against the background of the general mentality of the early church. And the first stage of movement will consist in the way the early Christians conceived their tradition at a time when they saw it as a message to live by and hand on, and not yet as the very word of God. The basic sources for this twofold study are obviously the writings of the New Testament, and so we take our stand in history around A.D. 51. But our direct sources will be, as much as possible, the research and interpretation done by others on those writings, and this will enable us to penetrate to some extent into the dark period of the preceding generation.

1. The Original Situation

Rudolf Bultmann begins his theology of the New Testament by saying: *"The message of Jesus* is a presupposition for the theology of the New Testament rather than a part of that theology itself."* So he devotes only one rather short chapter of his two-volume work to reconstructing that message: its focus on the reign of God as immediately impending, its insistence that the time has come and that this is the call to decision, its understanding of the demand of God as contrasted with Jewish legalism, its own ethic as formulated in the demand for love, and its conception of God as the real meaning of the eschatological message.[1]

7

Bultmann's next chapter reconstructs the kerygma of the earliest church, which conceived itself as the congregation of the end-time, thus implicitly understanding Jesus as the eschatological occurrence. So the first disciples betook themselves to Jerusalem as the focal point of the coming reign of God, though the same belief in the approaching end governed their missionary activity too: They must hasten through the land to call Israel to repentance. As for practical everyday attitudes, the eschatological congregation did not regard itself as a new religion, but it did regard itself as the "true Israel," and so a question arose on its relation to the empirical Israel of history, becoming especially acute on the validity of the Jewish law and its necessity for Gentiles who wished to share in the salvation that belonged to the Jewish people. Out of such a general developmental history there emerged the realization of the church as a distinct body that had to determine for itself what offices might be appropriately instituted for the direction of an eschatological congregation. One such office was clearly the ministry of the word. Indeed, the concern of "the twelve" was above all to proclaim the word and guard the tradition in which the history that founded the congregation was preserved and made present. And Bultmann goes on to speak of the need that was felt as time went on for a certain regulation of life in the congregation and for further institutional forms for maintaining continuity.

His third chapter deals with the kerygma of the Hellenistic church aside from Paul, for it was this latter church rather than the Jewish-Christian that mediated the kerygma to Paul. Basic in the missionary preaching to the Gentile world is the message of the one God, and the characterization of this world as sunk in ignorance and error, so that accepting the Christian faith is coming "to know God" and "the truth." Further, since there is a causal connection between heathen notions of God and heathen degradation in sin, the call to believe in the one true God is simultaneously a call to repentance, with a basis in the fact that God the Creator is also the Judge. This involved the preaching of the resurrection of the dead, who also are to be brought to account for their former deeds. And so the christological motif is an integral part of this kerygma: Jesus Christ appears at God's side as Judge, as God's representative and plenipotentiary. Not only as Judge, however; also as Savior for those who believe. Now this eschatological Judge and Savior is the crucified Jesus whom God raised from the dead; so the resurrection of Jesus is a basic constituent of the Hellenistic kerygma.

Bultmann continues with further motifs (I have given the headings of only one of the seven sections of his third chapter), but he has provided a sketch of history sufficient to bring us up to the period when our documents begin and enable us to make an empirical study of the origins of the Christian word. Against this general background in the middle of the 1st century, I wish now to set the materials that pertain to that study. The purpose is a general sketch, a kind of rough inventory, an overall view that, though static, will be the immediate context for a concentration on what was going forward. For such a purpose we can hardly do better than cite a key text in a letter that Paul wrote around A.D. 56:

> And now, my brothers, I must remind you of the gospel that I preached to you; the gospel which you received, on which you have taken your stand, and which is now bringing you salvation. Do you still hold fast the Gospel as I preached it to you? If not, your conversion was in vain.
>
> First and foremost, I handed on to you the facts which had been imparted to me: that Christ died for our sins, in accordance with the scriptures; that he was buried; that he was raised to life on the third day, according to the scriptures; and that he appeared to Cephas, and afterwards to the Twelve. Then he appeared to over five hundred of our brothers at once, most of whom are still alive, though some have died. Then he appeared to James, and afterwards to all the apostles (1 Cor. 15:1-7).

If this passage is subjected to analysis and the elements arranged schematically according to the divisions and subdivisions of a general concept of communication, we find that we have an extraordinarily comprehensive list with factors representative of practically all the significant components of such a concept.

Thus, we have at the focal point the content of the message communicated, which is designated (by the translator) as the "facts" about Jesus, and is summarily indicated as the message of his death, burial, resurrection, and appearance after death.

We have the link between the message and the Jewish traditions that are a source of interpretation and a criterion for assessment: The events narrated took place "according to the scriptures." We are introduced to the agents of the message: Paul himself, those who relayed it to him, but above all Peter, the Twelve, and the others who could vouch for the truth of the "facts" related. The activities of these agents are specified in what we know from other passages to be technical terms: gospeling ("the gospel that I preached" is literally "the gospel that I gospeled") and handing on. There is reference, finally, to those who received the message: the Corinthians addressed by Paul, and Paul himself at an earlier stage; to the manner in which they received it: through a conversion of heart and with a commitment to hold it fast; and to the effect it had on them: bringing them salvation.

In other words, if we think schematically but comprehensively of the content and act of communication, with subheadings for the first in terms of historical antecedents, narrative material, and form, and subheadings for the second in terms of agents and recipients of the communication, the media used for its communication, and the manner in which it is transmitted and received, then we find there are few elements in the list that are not represented in this one rich passage. I propose, then, to use this conceptual framework, not as if it were the structure of a biblical theology or of Paul's mind, but simply as a convenient means of structuring our own minds and listing the materials that pertain to the origins of the Christian word.[2]

Our first heading will be the content of the message, which divides at once into a doctrinal part and an ethical. If we accept Dodd's views as at least a fair approximation to the facts in regard to early usage, we may apply to these areas the technical terms of *kêrygma* and *didachê*, preaching or proclamation, and teaching. The kerygma would be quite simply the good news, recounting the life and work of Jesus Christ, his suffering and death, his resurrection from the dead, and all this as the climax of the divinely guided history of Israel. The teaching would follow in a second phase: Those who responded to the message of the kerygma would be instructed in the way of the Christians and the obligations of the Christian life, the technical term for this instruction being *catêchêsis*.[3]

Most of this book will focus on the content of the Christian message, so we may leave that heading for the moment and turn to the agents who communicated the message. A fairly comprehensive inventory can be made from the frequent lists of gifts, ministries, and offices in the New Testament. Thus, Ephesians (4:11) mentions apostles, prophets, evangelizers (let us reserve "evangelist" for the authors of the four canonical gospels), pastors, and teachers. Other lists and supplementary passages enable us to add the following: speakers, ecstatics and their interpreters, discerners (1 Cor. 12:8-10), administrators (deacons), leaders (Rom. 12:7-8), catechists (Gal. 6:6), counselors (1 Thess. 5:12), sages (Mt. 23:34), witnesses (Acts 1:22 and passim), and heralds (1 Tim. 2:7; 2 Tim. 1:11). To these we may add bishops (Acts 20:28) and elders (Acts 20:17). One cannot say that in every case there is question of an office technically conceived, for sometimes the participial form of the verb is used and there is emphasis on the activity rather than on the agent ("catechist" is literally "the one catechizing"); but they are open to such an interpretation and sometimes actually developed in that direction. There is question too of the extent to which, in the exercise of these "offices," there was concern directly with the communication of the message; in some cases this communication is at the center of the office, in others it is on the margins.

The various activities of these agents of the word are almost all either implicit in the title when it is a noun-form, or explicit in the operation when it is a verb-form; gospeling or evangelizing, preaching or heralding, teaching, catechizing, interpreting, etc. However, one technical term of considerable importance is not covered by the previous list. It is that of handing on, the notion more familiar to theology as "tradition." *Paradidonai* had a long history in Judaism; it was a key means of communicating the New Testament message, and a complex theology grew up around the idea, linking it with various acts of handing over in the life, death, and reign of Jesus, including the very act of the Father in handing over his Son (Rom. 8:32; see 4:25). But we have no word for the agent, except in the sense in which the unhappy Judas was a *traditor*. There does not seem, indeed, to have been an individual agent where the communication of the word was concerned; the "tradition" or "traditions" were bound up with the life of the community as community.[4]

It widens the view to turn from technical terms to the

everyday media of communication. Statistically, the simple act of speaking is far out in front as such a medium. Five verbs for speaking (*legô*, *laleô*, *eipon*, *erô*, *phêmi*) are together used over twenty-seven hundred times, and there are verbs of similar meaning used with lesser frequency, as well as words meaning to reply, contradict, argue, prove, etc. Then there is the act of writing, taken again in the everyday sense of the term and not at all in the technical and highly theological sense of "scripture." Thus, when Paul mentions his purpose "in writing this letter" (2 Cor. 13:10), his usage does not seem to involve a special theological significance. He is aware that his gift is operative in his writing too (Rom. 15:15), but this merely serves to show how integrated all his activities were with the grace he had received. It is important to notice this everyday aspect of the New Testament "media," for the tendency of controversy has been to inflate their meaning when convenient. Thus, Paul urged his readers to "hold fast to the traditions which you have learned from us by word or by letter" (2 Thess. 2:15), and these two, word and letter, have been turned into the scripture/tradition pair of later polemics. The tendency errs in two ways: by turning a casual use into one that is theologically charged, and by fixing attention too exclusively on the oral and written modes of communication.

The manner in which the agent of the message worked, the inner resources he could draw on, the attitude he showed toward his flock, this also is relevant to a view of communication. This is already clear in Paul's first letter. To begin with, he is *God's* agent, speaking "in the power of the Holy Spirit" (1 Thess. 1:5), "by the help of our God" (2:2), who had approved him "as fit to be entrusted with the Gospel" (2:4). On his side there is a corresponding faith and zeal, so that he brought the gospel "with strong conviction" (1:5), declaring it "frankly and fearlessly" (2:2), without deceit, greed, or ambition, with complete sincerity (2:3-7). All this simply reflects a more basic mode of being, which Paul regarded as part of bearing the message: "That is the kind of men we were at Thessalonica, and it was for your sake" (1:5). His concern for his flock is very much a factor: "With such yearning love we chose to impart to you not only the gospel of God but our very selves" (2:8). So is the burden of his work, in which he labored with his hands rather than be a charge on his church: "Remember, brothers, how we toiled and drudged" (2:9). The full story would be as extensive as Paul's biography; let these indications stand for the whole.

The recipients of the message are, in general, the unexpected. As Paul tells the Corinthians, not too delicately: You are nobodies. "Few of you are men of wisdom . . . few are powerful or highly born. Yet . . . God has chosen . . . things low and contemptible, mere nothings, to overthrow the existing order" (1 Cor. 1:26-28). Ephesians will give a classic description of the "former condition" of those called to hear the message: "without hope and without God" (2:11-12; see vv. 3-5). Paul himself was a very unlikely candidate, by any human standards, for hearing the Christian message (Gal. 1:13-16). So had been the ones Jesus chose for his disciples, as later accounts would make clear (Mk. 1:16-20). In fact, Jesus is described as consorting with "tax-gatherers and sinners" (Mk. 2:16).

Theologically, the two significant categories under this heading were Jew and Gentile. The decision to extend the word to the Gentiles was obviously agonizing, as appears even years later from the long explanation and elaborate justification given in Acts 6-11. The struggle was at its height in Paul's own time, and he wrestles with the problem that God seemed to have abandoned his people for the Gentiles (Romans 9-11). But Paul was already quite clear on the basic tenet, that no such categories mattered in the least: "There is no such thing as Jew and Greek, slave and freeman, male and female" (Gal. 3:28). As Matthew will have the Lord say: "Go forth . . . and make all nations my disciples" (28:19); and a much later writer: It is God's will "that all men should find salvation and come to know the truth" (1 Tim. 2:4).

On the manner of receiving the word, our last heading, 1 Thessalonians gives a wealth of data: "We call to mind . . . how your faith has shown itself in action, your love in labour, and your hope of our Lord Jesus Christ in fortitude" (1:3). Paul's visit to this church had not been fruitless, but "the welcome you gave the message meant grave suffering for you" (1:6). The effect of this visit is set forth in a classic description of their conversion: "how you turned from idols, to be servants of the living and true God, and to wait expectantly for the appearance from heaven of his Son Jesus, whom he raised from the dead" (1:9-10). Their state, however, was not one of mere waiting for the end of their world; Paul appealed to them "to live lives worthy of the God who calls you into his kingdom and glory" (2:12), "to stand firm for the faith" (3:2). He had passed on to them the way they "must live to please God" (4:1), and speaks of the orders he had given them in the name of the Lord (4:2). For God had called them to holiness (4:7), and taught them to love one another (4:9).

Drawing elements from other writings for a summary view, we may say that the message is a call (2 Thess. 1:11) by the choice of God (1 Thess. 1:4), to which the one called owed obedience (2 Thess. 1:8) in faith (Rom. 10:8). Indeed the message can be called the word of hearing or obedience (*logon akoês*, 1 Thess. 2:13). We may end this section of the chapter with a passage from Romans that complements the classic text of 1 Corinthians with which we began; each in its way provides the materials for a New Testament theology of the word and its communication:

> How could they invoke one in whom they had no faith? And how could they have faith in one they had never heard of? And how hear without someone to spread the news? And how could anyone spread the news without a commission to do so? And that is what Scripture affirms: "How welcome are the feet of the messengers of good news!"
> But not all have responded to the good news (Rom. 10:13-16).

2. The Original Thematization

Our first section was mainly an inventory of New Testament materials for a theology of the word, organized statically according to a conceptual system. But our purpose is not a static organization; quite the contrary, it is the ongoing path of history. The first steps along that path are fateful in a high degree, as determining the direction of advance; they are also extremely difficult, as may be symbolized by a simple experience. One spring the melting snows revealed in the lawn beneath my window the maze of interconnecting paths that the mice had burrowed through the grass during the winter. There was no pattern discernible to the casual eye, no beginning, no end, no direction, no sequence—just an irregular network, an unstructured grid, an extravagance of crisscrossing. With some exaggeration I suggest this as an image of the original situation in the history I am writing. There is a tangled complex of ideas: gospel, preaching, teaching, tradition, catechesis, prophecy, interpretation, witness, discipleship, apostleship, and hundreds, literally hundreds, of others.[5] One can organize them artificially in order to make a rough inventory. But that does not initiate the forward movement of history, or even give the direction of advance. Where is the point of departure, what is the direction to take, and how do we initiate the movement?

With the problem defined in this way, we begin. For this first step, if we are not just to cast about in trial and error, we need some sort of clue, and I suggest that the clue is provided in the very phrase we have been using to describe our topic, the Christian word of God. I do not mean that the clue is found in the content of the term; that simply adds one more to the tangled nest already formed by gospel, preaching, teaching, tradition, catechesis, and the rest. The clue is in the act of naming the relevant materials the word of God. There is a thematizing here, that thematizing is an event, and the event carries us forward and sets us on a path through history. At some point in time, and in some discrete occurrence, the materials about which we have been talking came to be recognized as the word of God. If we can locate that occurrence, and study the materials before and after the event, we will be launched on the path we are searching for. I believe that it is relatively simple to conclude to such a transition, and to describe both the "before" and "after" stages of history; though we cannot locate the point of transition with the accuracy we would desire, there is still sufficient clarity to structure our first two chapters.

This act of "naming" a topic for theological reflection, of thematizing a set of materials under a certain aspect, brings into focus the point often made about the selective process of history. Realities exist before they are named, and the naming generally points only to a certain aspect that does not by any means exhaust the reality. Isaac, which means "He laughed," does not have his whole being revealed in the fact that God's word to

Abraham promising a son occasioned laughter (Gen. 17:17-19). So a naming and a thematizing each has a negative as well as positive side. Positively, it means an enrichment of our understanding; when applied to objects, it creates the possibility of a developing science, of penetrating more and more deeply into the heart of the matter. But, negatively, since it means at the same time a selection of an aspect from the rich diversity of the materials, it condemns some of them to almost certain neglect.[6]

In the same way, to name a certain reality "the word of God" was also an act of thematizing. The reality already existed; it existed in the rich life of the Christian community and the diverse activities by which that community tried to assimilate, put into practice, and hand on what it had received from Jesus and his first disciples. When the rich and diversified materials that constituted this reality came to be known as the word of God, both loss and gain resulted. There was gain in the new insight achieved, in the recognition of God's part in all this activity, in the deepening penetration of the mystery of his dealings with his children. But there was loss in the resulting tendency to leave the human element in the background. As the definition of the divinity of Christ led almost inevitably to neglect of his humanity, so the idea that God had spoken to his people in the Christian message led the church to neglect the human agents of the message and the particular cultural situations in which communication of the message to human receivers took place.

Of course, when I speak of naming the materials "the word of God" and thus introducing a theme for thought, I am not denying that there were names prior to that event, which themselves constituted a thematization; it is, in fact, my purpose at the moment to discover what those early designations were. We anticipate our second chapter, then, to say that the message had been thematized as the word of God by the time of the Acts of the Apostles; we use this thematizing to structure our first two stages; and we ask: How were the materials that pertain to the Christian word commonly designated in the period prior to their becoming known as the word of God? Our answer will be that the earlier designations were "gospel," or "kerygma," or "message." It may even be that, at one stage, there was no thematic designation: One simply referred to "what has been handed on," or to "what happened in the life and times of Jesus."

In regard to "gospel," it is clear enough that it was an early designation for the Christian message and then dropped out of usage in some of the later writings. I have already quoted a passage from Paul that is widely recognized as a key text for the early history of the message. Recall the opening lines:

> And now, my brothers, I must remind you of the gospel that I preached to you; the gospel which you received, on which you have taken your stand, and which is now bringing you salvation. Do you still hold fast the Gospel as I preached it to you? (1 Cor. 15:1-2).

Here, in a letter written around A.D. 56, and in a passage considered to give the core of the Christian message, we have an especially emphatic use of the term "gospel." In fact, the verb and its object are cognate in the first verse, which reads literally, "the gospel that I gospeled to you." But, though the usage is especially emphatic here, it is not at all singular; it agrees completely with Paul's general practice. In the very letter that first applies "word of God" to the Christian message, he has already five times designated that message as "gospel" (1 Thess. 1:5; 2:2, 4, 8, 9). Further, the total number of occurrences in his writings tells the same story: The verb-form of "gospel" is found some eighteen times and the noun-form some fifty-seven times.[7] In contrast the number drops in the synoptic gospels (Mark uses the noun seven times, Luke's gospel uses the verb ten times, Matthew uses the noun four times and the verb once), and disappears entirely in John's gospel and letters. It does seem that for the first of our New Testament writers "gospel" is a key word, one of his ways of thematizing the message, while for the very late writers it is not a key word at all.

There is a parallel history for the term "kerygma," and its verb-form, *kêryssein*. The noun-form, for Paul, is a close companion to "gospel" (so much so that the New English Bible regularly translates it by that word). Thus, he associates these two words in the phrase "according to the Gospel I brought you and the proclamation (*kêrygma*) of Jesus Christ" (Rom. 16:25). Now this form, after occurring four times in Paul, and putting in an appearance in both Matthew and Luke, simply drops from sight in John. The verb-form, more important insofar as the notion involved puts more emphasis on the activity than on the content,[8] is also associated with "gospel," often having that noun as its direct object; now the verb too has its history: It occurs some fifteen times in Paul, maintains the pace in the synoptic writers (including Acts here), and once again drops completely out of sight in John's gospel and letters.

There is surely no mystery about this, which corresponds to quite normal psychological patterns. A man may be full of enthusiasm at having won a woman as his bride, but with the passing of time, even though his love does not diminish, his mood becomes one of quiet joy; the event has passed to be succeeded by a settled state. Similarly, a religious community forms in the enthusiasm of an event, but, as time passes, with a new generation inheriting the wealth of tradition instead of creating or discovering it, the situation changes. You cannot be forever bursting with the good news, and there is something distinctly artificial in the efforts of modern "evangelical" preachers who would try it. Paul then, so close to the early years of Christianity and to his own remarkable conversion, was deeply conscious both of the sensational event that the Christian word was in his world and of his own overpowering need to bring it to others. The synoptics would have recovered something of the sensation that the Lord Jesus was in his person and his ministry. But with the establishment of the church the explosive effect of the good news was bound to subside, the institutionalizing of the faith would bring classes like elders, bishops, deacons, to the fore, and the daily routine of a peaceful abiding in Christ (realized eschatology) would replace the first rapturous welcome. Thus, the "evangelizer" in the original sense of gospeler and the herald, the *kêryx*, would recede into the background.

But the question inevitably arises about the earlier history of the message: Were the terms "gospel" and "kerygma" first on the scene? or do they themselves already represent a thematizing of the original Christian message, which would then have existed previously under some other name or under no name at all? One surmises that they were not the earliest terms in use, if for no other reason than that we can hardly imagine the holy women delivering their account of the Easter event under those titles. Years later Matthew will describe them as running from the tomb to "announce" (*apaggeilai*, 28:8; see also Lk. 24:9) their experience, but their "story" (*ta rêmata tauta*, Lk. 24:11) was regarded as nonsense. A firmer basis for an educated guess is found in the derivation of these terms from the Old Testament; here there is a rich background, especially for the concept of good news and of the messenger who brings it:

> All Jerusalem stands on the towers and walls expecting the train of returning exiles. Then they see the messenger. . . . He proclaims the victory of Yahweh over the whole world. Yahweh is now returning to Sion to rule. The messenger publishes it, and the new age begins . . . Salvation comes with the word of proclamation.[9]

This account of the good news that Old Testament Israel experienced (the reference is to such texts as Isaiah 52:7) would explain the adoption of the term "gospel" to describe the New Testament message. But the Old Testament did not become available overnight to explain the Christian event and the Christian doctrine; rather, there was prolonged searching of the scriptures to find the relevant passages.[10] In the present state, therefore, of research and interpretation I cannot find even a reasonably probable path for the word "gospel" from John the Baptist and Jesus through the early church to Paul, or attempt to fix the point in time when the usage taken for granted in Paul became established.

We can be a little more positive in suggesting that another early designation of the Christian word was the term *logos*. But it is important to translate this term simply as "message" and not as "word." The latter rendering, through an inevitable association of ideas, will be linked with the word *of God*, and thus provided with a content beyond what seems to have been intended originally. In Paul's letters at least, the original meaning could sometimes be quite simply "the message," and the New English Bible will render this generic sense in a variety of ways: "The welcome you gave the *message* meant grave suffering for you" (1 Thess. 1:6); "When anyone is under instruction in the *faith*" (Gal. 6:6); "that God may give us an opening for *preaching*" (Col. 4:3). The specific content of this word is never far from mind, as appears both from the context of these passages and from the various qualifiers that are used elsewhere: the word "of the cross" (1 Cor. 1:18), the word "of reconciliation" (2 Cor. 5:19), the word "of Christ" (Col. 3:16). But there does seem to be one rather undetermined, generic sense that may be translated variously by message, faith, preaching; and this, in that early period of Christian history that is represented by Paul's writings.

Can we penetrate even further backwards and reach a time when, as seems a priori likely, there was no designation at all for the message? There is indeed a remarkable usage in Acts where the author speaks of "the facts about Jesus" (18:25; see also 28:31; and 1:3 in regard to the kingdom); now there is no word in Greek to correspond to the translator's "facts": there is simply *ta peri tou Iêsou*. This is a relatively late work; does the usage here reflect a relatively early practice? Conzelmann is of the contrary view: The message is now so well known that only this hint is needed.[11] One must respect this view; at the same time, new history requires ever new research and new effort at interpretation. In any case there is a parallel to Luke's use (the neuter plural of the article) in two occurrences of the relative pronoun in Paul. In one passage he would instruct the Corinthians on the Eucharist and wrote (in literal translation): "For I received from the Lord *what* I delivered to you" (1 Cor. 11:23); in the other, he is reminding them of the gospel message and wrote (again literally): "I delivered to you *what* I also received" (1 Cor. 15:3). Finally, we may reflect on present practice when news is going round: "Did you hear what they're saying?" "There's a report out of Ottawa. . . ." "I heard an amazing story on the radio. . . ." In some such wholly untechnical terms, surely, the Christian message would receive its first name and designation.

I have listed some of the chief ways in which the early church, especially as it is represented by Paul, conceived what I vaguely referred to earlier as "the materials" we are studying, what we will later refer to as "the Christian word of God." It will be useful to settle on a term to describe this stage at the beginning of our history, and I know of no better one than simply "message." As Dodd says, beginning one of the last papers of his remarkable career, "The term 'message' has been chosen as the most comprehensive term available for the whole range of that which it is the business of the Christian ministry to convey to the faithful and to the world in general so far as it will hear."[12] With this presentation of the early period of that message, I think we have set the stage for the first great transition in our history, and made it possible to see as a real event in time the emergence of the characterization of the message as the word of God.

CHAPTER TWO

THE CHRISTIAN MESSAGE AS THE WORD OF GOD

The sequence here is based on the hypothesis that the Christian message, which we now know as the word of God and take for granted under that heading, was not originally so conceived, but was simply the joyful message, the good news of salvation in Christ; only later did it come to be known as the word of God. There is a *prima facie* case for that hypothesis in the evident difference between the way the communication of the holy women was received on the first Easter and the attitude that Luke takes toward the same message sixty years later. The story the women told on returning from the tomb is regarded as a babbling and incoherent account of some experience they may have had. Sixty years later Luke takes it for granted that this story, now greatly expanded but built round the same nucleus, is quite simply the word of God; as he has Paul and Barnabas declare to the Jews of Pisidian Antioch: "It was necessary . . . that the word of God should be declared to you first" (Acts 13:46).

However, that *prima facie* case must be substantiated by more thorough examination of the situation before and after the transition to the new conception; and, if we cannot pinpoint the event itself of the transition, we have at least to raise the question of its time, place, and circumstances. Further, there is a special need in this chapter to notice the fact that we are not dealing merely with the *content* of the message when it is specified as the word of God. Beyond that, the very *act of utterance* is specified as God's activity; and this second aspect will have its own fateful role to play in the history of the word. Accordingly, this chapter will be divided into two parts, to deal first with the transition from message to word of God, and then with the notion of God as active in the communication of his word.

22

1. Transition from "Message" to "Word of God"

The question here is: When and where and how did the message, which was known as the gospel or simply as the Christian message, come to be thought of as the word of God? There was, we are led to believe, a distinct change in the thinking of the early church; gradually or suddenly, but under determined circumstances, a mere narrative of men and women was transformed, in reality or in the understanding of the reality, into the word of God. From the viewpoint of history that I have adopted, it is important to try to trace that transition.

The tentative conclusion that I have reached may be expressed as follows: Luke's theology, especially as revealed in his Acts of the Apostles, represents a stage at which the Christian message is firmly established as the word of God; Paul's theology represents the situation a generation earlier when the breakthrough to conceiving the message as word of God has been made but not yet exploited, when the conception has not yet become so familiar as to be taken for granted in the thinking of the early believers. These two stages will serve as a structure to guide our investigation and as a context in which to study consequent developments.

As a preliminary, recall briefly the notion of the word of God as it was conceived when the Christian message began. "The word of the Lord" is so frequently used in the Old Testament that we may forget that it is only one of many media of divine revelation and that, like all religious notions, it has a history. In fact, it emerges as the dominant one from a complex assortment of media: Nature and natural phenomena, casting lots and divination, dreams and chance experiences, history and visions, all of these mingle with the word as means for learning about God and his holy will.[1] In time, however, Old Testament religion emerged as primarily a religion of the word of God. This emergence may have had its origins in the context of the prophets, as a Protestant author believes,[2] or in that of the law spoken by God from Sinai, as a Catholic author maintains,[3] but eventually the prophet stands out as the organ *par excellence* of the word. Jeremiah will serve as illustration: "The words of Jeremiah. . . . The word of the LORD came to him" (1:1-2); and six more times in the short first chapter we have "the word of the LORD" or some equivalent phrase.

The content of this word is basically history. That is true, where we might least expect it, of the prophetic word itself: "The Prophets were above all commentators on history."[4] The great events of Israel's past, the mighty acts of God, these were the theme of both chronicler and prophet. Of course, there were also songs, prayers, edifying fables, proverbs, applications to life and conduct; but all this gathered round the historical core of events in which God revealed his will and character. Yet the word did not merely interpret history, it also effected it. The word of God has an efficacy linked to the fact that very often it is a command. The command goes forth to the universe, and the universe responds: "God said, 'Let there be light,' and there was light" (Gen. 1:3). A similar power is attributed to the words of men, especially when they deliver curses or blessings: They go forth from the speaker as realities in their own right. This belief probably facilitated that later personification of the word which was linked also with Stoic influence. By steps the divine attributes, especially Wisdom and the Word, came to be conceived as intermediaries between God and the world. Thus Philo could speak of the *Logos* as the pattern and instrument of God in creation, as God's first-born Son, his image and shadow, as indeed *theos* though not *ho theos*.[5]

The notion of the written word of God was slow to form. Naturally so, since written language was itself a late cultural phenomenon. The decisive period for the cultural step was taken in the 11th and 10th centuries, with compositions on the early kingdom and the preceding period, and the establishment of archives. The next step was to push back into the dim past of patriarchal times and the exodus. In a third step, from the 8th to the 6th centuries, the prophets spoke their mighty words, some of which were preserved, often fragmentarily, in writing. The time of disasters led to meditation on the past, and a reediting of the texts under "deuteronomic" and "sacerdotal" influences. In the time of the Persians sapiential writings flourished, and "edifying tales" like that of Judith. Finally, the painful experience of reduction to a province opened minds to possibilities beyond those of history, and apocalyptic literature like the book of Daniel appeared.[6]

With writing then lagging far behind the spoken word as a

phenomenon, it was normal that the notion of these writings as word of God should only slowly come to formulation. Chapter 36 of Jeremiah shows how the written word was held in awe, though even here the people *hear* the word as it is read aloud to them. It was only after the exile that the "Jews became the people of the book, and that book Deuteronomy."[7] And the first mention of "sacred books" does not occur till far on in history: "Our support is the holy books in our possession" (1 Mach. 12:9).

What developed slowly in Old Testament times is simply taken for granted in the New Testament where prophecy and the scriptures are reverenced equally as the word of God. Sometimes the picture for the spoken word shows God speaking to a chosen leader, as he spoke to Moses (Rom. 9:15; Heb. 8:5; Jn. 9:29); more often God speaks through the prophet to a wider audience: "All this happened in order to fulfil what the Lord declared through the prophet" (Mt. 1:22). Similarly, it is taken for granted that the scriptures are the word of God: Just as we have "the prophet says," so we have "Scripture says" (Jn. 7:38), or "it is written" (Mt. 4:4, rendered in NEB: "Scripture says"). We have the scriptures giving testimony (Jn. 5:39) or foreseeing what would happen (Gal. 3:8), and in general there is an ease in passing back and forth between "God says" and "scripture says" that argues identification of the two ideas, though it may be that the introduction of the Christian word begins to disturb in some slight measure the identity that prevailed at first between "word of God" and "the scriptures." Finally, we have the idea of the inspiration of the scriptures and of the impulse of the Holy Spirit at work in the prophets—of which more in the second part of this chapter.

We should notice, before turning to the Christian message, that the New Testament did not take over without modification the Jewish view of God's word; there is a change in at least two ways. First, a new perspective colors now the whole of the Old Testament, prophecy and scripture, bringing out a hitherto hidden pattern; it becomes a Christian book, declaring in its own way the Christian gospel: "This gospel God announced beforehand in sacred scripture through his prophets" (Rom. 1:2; see 16:25-26). According to Luke it is Jesus himself to whom this new perspective is due: "Then he began with Moses and all the prophets, and explained to them the passages which referred to himself in every part of the scriptures" (Lk. 24:27). The other change is in contrast with this: There seems to be a certain awkwardness, once the Christian message is regarded as the word of God, in using the same term for the Old Testament message; if I am correct in this, it is a remarkable fact, and I shall come back to it presently.

The immediate and difficult task, however, is to try to trace the steps by which this notion of the word of God, so highly reverenced by the Jewish people and consequently by the early church, came to be applied to the Christian message. The magnitude of the step is phenomenal, though it easily escapes us as we go through the Acts and find Luke inserting it, as if it were ready-made for the purpose, into his account of the early preaching. But there is a giant leap from the babblings of the holy women at Easter to this concept, comparable, I think, to the transition by which Jesus the Proclaimer became Jesus the Proclaimed. We have studies in abundance of that latter leap but still await one of the former; meanwhile I must make do with my surmises.

Let us start where the ground is solid. In A.D. 51 Paul wrote what is commonly regarded as the earliest extant New Testament document, his first letter to the Thessalonians. After the salutation he thanks God for the good results of his preaching at Thessalonica, speaks of the persecution the church there had suffered, and answers the calumnies that had been directed against him in that community. In this context Paul insists that he did not preach merely his own views or doctrines: "This is why we thank God continually, because when we handed on God's message, you received it, not as the word of men, but as what it truly is, the very word of God at work in you who hold the faith" (1 Thess. 2:13). The whole sequence of his argument up to this point makes it clear that he is speaking of the Christian message, the gospel that he had brought and they had welcomed. So here, about twenty years after the beginning of the Christian message, we have the first documented instance of the application to it of the term "word of God."

Is it possible that in this very passage we are assisting at the first emergence of the usage? that here Paul brings to formulation for the first time the notion that this gospel, this message, this account of the saving facts about Jesus that the church had preached for twenty years, is to be considered the word of God? There is in fact a certain awkwardness in Paul's language that has to be explained; a literal translation might run, "receiving speech of hearing from us of God you accepted not speech of man but as it really is speech of God." (I translate *logos* by "speech," for we can use that word in English without the article, as Paul uses *logos*.) It seems possible to explain the awkwardness by supposing that Paul is introducing a new idea that he himself has hardly thought of up till now. There is a given reality that has been conceived prior to this as the gospel, and Paul is carried along by the momentum of his thought to realize suddenly that this reality deserves the same reverence that all his life he has shown toward the word of prophet and scripture. There would thus be two moments of thought in this one passage with regard to the term *logos* and a free paraphrase might run: When you received the *message* that was preached by us but comes from God, you accepted it . . . as the very *word* of God.

However, a possible explanation falls far short of a verified position, and I leave the determination of the question to the experts. Restricting ourselves to what is clear to the nonspecialist, we can at least say that "word of God" is not at this time Paul's spontaneous way of conceiving the message; five times already in this letter he has referred to it rather as the "gospel," and that surely indicates a spontaneity that seemed to be lacking in the awkward text I quoted. Neither does "word of God" take over from this time forward as his favorite designation; in all his writings there are only five other texts (1 Cor. 14:36; 2 Cor. 2:17; 4:2; Phil. 1:14; Col. 1:25) where the phrase may refer to the Christian message, and in only one of them does this reference approach 1 Thessalonians in clarity (Phil. 1:14). It does seem as if the usage did not enter deeply into Paul's thought-patterns, but rather came to him on the spur of the moment as he wrote to the Thessalonians, and even proved a little difficult to integrate with his previous usage of the term.

Nevertheless, 1 Thessalonians, 2:13, testifies that an event of great importance did occur; whenever, wherever, however it happened, there is a new idea in the Christian universe of thought. It challenges us to investigate its emergence. I suggest the following line of thought: There are three related phrases that crop up in Paul's writings, the word, the word of the Lord, the word of God. All three, it happens, are found in the opening paragraphs of 1 Thessalonians: The welcome this church gave the *word* meant suffering for them (1:6); from Thessalonica the *word of the Lord* rang out (1:8); and the message Paul gave them is the very *word of God* (2:13). There is an obvious progression in thought from first to third; that may be simply accidental here, but my surmise is that they may also have emerged into Christian consciousness in just that order, with transition to the second helped along by one ambiguity, and transition to the third by another.

"The word" is used in Paul, simply and without addition, to designate the gospel; it is the usage referred to in my first chapter as the most generic way of designating what he had received and is handing on: the message. Thus, he speaks of one who is a catechumen of the word (Gal. 6:6); he asks for prayers that God may open the door of the word, to tell the secret of Christ (Col. 4:3). But it was easy and natural to add various adjectival phrases: the word of the cross (1 Cor. 1:18), the word of reconciliation (2 Cor. 5:19), the word of life (Phil. 2:16). Most important of all, it was easy and natural to speak of the word of Christ (Col. 3:16; compare Rom. 10:17); but that phrase is generally recognized to be ambiguous—it may mean the word that comes from Christ, or it may mean the word about Christ.

Now Paul's standard title for Christ is "the Lord," so transition to "the word of the Lord" would be quite normal, and this phrase would carry with it the ambiguity of "the word of Christ." There are, it is true, only three occurrences of "word of the Lord" in Paul. One we already saw: "From Thessalonica the word of the Lord rang out" (1 Thess. 1:8). Later in the same letter there is a second, referring to a specific item in the message: "For this we tell you as the Lord's word: we who are left alive . . . shall not forestall those who have died" (4:15). The third is again general: "And now . . . pray for us, that the word of the Lord may have everywhere the swift and glorious course that it has had among you" (2 Thess. 3:1). To these three, however, we may add equivalent usages, such as 1 Corinthians, 7:12, which we translate: "I say this, not the Lord" (see also 1 Cor. 7:10; 9:14; 14:37).

The five occurrences in Paul of "word of God" for the Christian message have already been noted. It remains simply to add that the ambiguity of "Lord" would facilitate transition to this third phrase. Study of New Testament Christology reveals that what is attributed to Yahweh, the "Lord" of the Old Testament, is transferred to the "Lord" Jesus in the New, so that one has always to determine whether "Lord" refers to *ho theos*, the God of Israel, or to his Son. Thus, in Romans 10, 9-17, Paul passes back and forth from the Lord Jesus to the Lord of the Old Testament. So it is that a double ambiguity is operative, one between subjective and objective in "word of Christ" and in "word of the Lord" (this too is found in Romans 10), and another between "Lord" understood of Jesus and "Lord" understood of Yahweh. With the help of this double ambiguity the Christian message may have come to be known as the word of God.

Does it go without stressing that I cannot be satisfied with my surmises on the origin of 1 Thessalonians, 2:13? My hope is simply that I have raised a significant question for investigation by those competent for the task. And I should like to recommend here also the question I postponed earlier: It seems worth noticing that Paul so rarely speaks simply and without qualification of the Old Testament as word of God. He will use the equivalent; he will speak of the word that is written (1 Cor. 15:54), and over and over will quote the Old Testament using the formula, "It is written," but perhaps only once does he speak of the word of God in a passage that clearly refers to the Old Testament (Rom. 9:6). If this turns out to be the case, it could mean that his breakthrough in 1 Thessalonians is working more effectively in his mind than otherwise appears; a new meaning of "word of God" is quietly replacing the old.

From Paul we turn to study the synoptic writers, not specifically their doctrine, but what happened in and through them to change doctrine and usage. From this viewpoint, the significant event in Matthew and Mark was that what Jesus had said in his life on earth came to be understood simply as the word; where Paul had thought mainly of a word about Jesus, they think of the word that Jesus himself spoke. And the significant event in Luke was that he took over the work of Mark and went beyond it to call the word of Jesus the word *of God*; then, in a further step taken in Acts, the word of the apostles about Jesus also came to be firmly established as the word of God. What was an innovation (as we surmise) in Paul, became domiciled in Luke.

Mark refers to what Jesus preached simply as "the word" (v.g., 2:2 and 4:33: *logos*, translated in NEB by "message"), and in fact reserves both *logos* and *rêma* almost exclusively for what Jesus said. We need not go through his gospel; the sufficient and truly remarkable passage is found in his parable of the sower, where he seven times has Jesus speak simply and absolutely of the word. The peculiarities of this usage have been observed by the New Testament scholars; thus Dodd remarks:

> Now this whole passage is strikingly unlike in language and style to the majority of the sayings of Jesus. Its vocabulary includes (within this short space) seven words which are not proper to the rest of the Synoptic record. All seven are characteristic of the vocabulary of Paul, and most of them occur also in other apostolic writers. These facts create at once a presumption that we have here not a part of the primitive tradition of the words of Jesus, but a piece of apostolic teaching.[8]

Jeremiah agrees and adds some details:

> . . . in this short passage a number of sayings about "the Word" occur, which are not found elsewhere in the teaching of Jesus, but on the other hand are common in the apostolic age: the preacher preaches the word; the word is received, and that with joy; persecution arises on account of the word, the word is a cause of stumbling, the word "grows," the word brings forth fruit.[9]

The point being made here is important for the movement of history: "The word" does not go back to Jesus as a designation for his message. Rather, it arises in the early church, mainly to designate the word about Jesus, and it is the church too that applies it to the word that Jesus himself spoke. Further we can notice a clear progress through the three synoptic gospels. Mark introduces the parable of the sower by saying, "To you the secret of the kingdom of God has been given" (4:11). Matthew, who follows Mark's usage on the word only in this parable, will speak here of the word of the kingdom (13:19). Finally, Luke will boldly write, "The seed is the word of God" (8:11).

It is Luke indeed who seems to be the real theologian of the word of God. Even his gospel shows a marked step forward, for it uses this term for the teaching of Jesus: "The people crowded upon him to listen to the word of God" (5:1). But the gospel, though it prepares us for the usage of Acts in many ways, does not mark the term of this development. That distinction belongs to the Acts of the Apostles, unquestionably so. Here we have the three forms we met in Paul, the word, the word of the Lord, and the word of God. They are used frequently and almost inter-changeably, as if the choice were merely random, with some sixteen occurrences of "the word" in reference to the gospel, some seven of "the word of the Lord," and some thirteen of "the word of God" (variant readings prevent the count from being more than rough). Most certainly this latter phrase, understood of the gospel, is now domiciled in the church.

All the wealth of previous writings seems to pour into Luke's usage here. There are the adjectival phrases: the word of this salvation (13:26), the word of his grace (14:3; 20:32), the word of the gospel (15:7). There is a quoted saying of Jesus, "We should keep in mind the words of the Lord Jesus . . . 'Happiness lies more in giving than in receiving' " (20:35). Various verbs have "the word" as direct object; often the verb is simply *speak* (*lalein*), but sometimes it is to *gospel* (8:4, etc.) and sometimes to *declare* (*kataggellein*, 13:5, etc.); once the word is *sent* (10:36), once Paul *teaches* it (18:11), and the apostles are at the *service* of the word (6:4). Again there are passages recalling "the swift and glorious course" of the word we saw in 2 Thessalonians, as when Luke writes: "The word of God now spread more and more widely" (6:7; see also 12:24 and 19:20). And there is a significant reference to the word that *happened* (10:37; the noun here is *rêma*).

Strange that in John's gospel the one occurrence of the term *ho logos tou theou* is in reference to the Old Testament (10:35; but see 1 Jn. 2:14); for the idea of the new word that God has spoken, is in fact speaking, fills the gospel. Overwhelmingly in John the word is a word of the Father or of Jesus. With Jesus it may refer to a particular word, but often *logos* refers to the message of Jesus in its totality. So much so that the New English Bible will translate it by such terms as "revelation" or "teaching": "If you dwell with the revelation (*logos*) I have brought, you are indeed my disciples" (8:31); "you are bent on killing me because my teaching (*logos*) makes no headway with you" (8:37). Sometimes there are distinct terms for the global meaning of Jesus' message and the language he uses: "Why do you not understand my language (*lalia*)? It is because my revelation (*logos*) is beyond your grasp" (8:43).[10] There is clearly a new depth of meaning in John's reference to the word of Jesus, and it becomes even more mystery-laden when he links Jesus' word to that of the Father. "And the word you hear is not mine: it is the word of the Father who sent me" (14:24, and passim in the gospel and first letter).

Finally, there is the most profoundly Johannine use of all, the Word-God of the prologue of the gospel. Not only have we the word of God that the apostles spoke about Jesus, and the word of God that Jesus himself spoke, but we have the Word-God that Jesus is: "When all things began, the Word already was. The Word dwelt with God, and what God was, the Word was. The Word, then, was with God at the beginning. . . . So the Word became flesh; he came to dwell among us" (1:1-2, 14). This usage is of the highest importance in a study of the word of God to men; it is in continuity with ideas we have already seen, but also it introduces a quite new dimension that is better taken up in chapter six.

The various nuances we find in the other New Testament writings, interesting though they be, do not seem to add transitions and changes of major importance, or to be of decisive significance for the history of the word. May I repeat that my purpose is to study what went forward. The perspective is quite different therefore from that of Kittel in his article on *legô* in the New Testament. In that enormously erudite study I suppose every occurrence of *logos* in the New Testament is noted and discussed, but the perspective is far more that of the unity of New Testament usage than of its diversity. Thus, for a large part of the New Testament he finds "an essentially uniform picture of usage and content"[11] and, even when he comes to the great advance made by John in the conception of Jesus as himself the

Word of God, he insists as much on the continuity as on the development:

> There is not the slightest difference, but full and unremitting correspondence with the fundamental NT fact constantly described herewith, if we say that Jesus is not just the One who brings the Word but the One who incorporates it in His person, in the historical process of His speech and action, of His life and being.[12]

For my purpose, on the contrary, it is change that matters. What is "essentially uniform" belongs to the routine and repetitive that we exclude from history; continuity in change is not denied, but it is subordinate to change itself.

However, there is one important step to be noticed before we leave this section: It is the addition of the New Testament as writings to the body of the scriptures. What were for a time the apostolic writings, and as such worthy of veneration, came to be put on the same footing with those books that the early church knew as the scriptures and we know as the Old Testament. We should neither exaggerate nor belittle this development. It would be easy to minimize it, for it is the inevitable consequence of the revolutionary step by which the gospel came to be recognized as the word of God: What was held of the spoken word was simply extended to the written word as well. Nevertheless, psychology does not operate with the smoothness of logic, and psychologically the step was difficult: "The scriptures" were an awesome and a holy reality to which one did not lightly add further material.

The hints found in the New Testament itself that some of its writings are on a par with "the scriptures" are therefore rather remarkable. When 2 Peter (3:16) speaks of the way some "ignorant and unstable" persons misinterpret passages in Paul's letters, "as they do *the other scriptures*," he seems to be taking a bold and innovative step. One could, however, argue that 2 Peter is not really ahead of his contemporaries; it is just that this letter is very late, a good deal later even than the date usually assigned to it. That is the position of Campenhausen, who regards it as post-Marcionite and dates it around the middle of the 2nd century.[13]

Campenhausen's own chronology of events runs as follows.

He regards Justin as among the last of those for whom the term "the scriptures" means quite simply the Old Testament.[14] He refers to a Basilidean treatise described by Hippolytus as quoting from the New Testament "scriptures,"[15] but his study concentrates on Marcion as the real author of the concept of the Christian bible.[16] Yet, even in the time of Ireneus the transition is not complete. Ireneus was indeed "the first catholic theologian who dared to adopt the Marcionite principle of a new 'scripture,' "[17] but the usage is not yet domiciled:

> As occasion requires he speaks simply of the fourfold Gospel, of the Acts of the Apostles, or of the letters of the Apostle. Sometimes he groups these books together with the Old Testament, and refers to the whole without differentiation by the long-hallowed names of "scriptures of the Lord" "the scriptures" or "the scripture." This does not, however, occur regularly, but only occasionally and almost as if by inadvertence. In general these terms—as also the solemn formulas of quotation—are still confined to the books of the Old Testament.[18]

It is to be noted also that the terms "Old Testament" and "New Testament" were unknown to Ireneus. This phraseology, which was the one thing lacking in the Muratorian fragment to complete the transition, is anticipated in Melito of Sardis, and comes closer to clear formulation in Clement of Alexandria and Origen. After this tentative period of formulation the usage was rapidly accepted, and "the scriptures" became what they have been ever since for the Christian believer, the books of Old and New Testaments.[19]

2. God Active in His Word

Besides content there is activity; the terms are correlatives. The word of God can therefore be conceived as a message that relates "the facts about Jesus" and other information pertaining to the content of the message, and this viewpoint was dominant in the first part of this chapter. But it can also be conceived as the active utterance of the message, and this aspect deserves separate treatment. True, it was never entirely out of sight in discussion of the content. Already in chapter one it appeared in the cognate structure of "gospeling the gospel," and it was still more to the fore in the notion of kerygma, which can mean the act of proclaiming as well as the message proclaimed. If it does not seem so close to the surface in "word of God," that is due to our Western habit of concentrating on the objective content of the word. The Hebrew way of thinking is different. As Kittel says, beginning his study of Jesus as the Word: "At the head of the train of thought sketched by the term *logos* there stands, not a concept, but the event which has taken place, and in which God declares Himself, causing His Word to be enacted."[20] And so we come to the word of God as "alive and active," "at work" in those who hold the faith; that is, we come to that aspect which refers to the activity of God himself in uttering his word.

However, we do not thereby separate God from prophet and sacred writer, for the word that is significant for history is the word that God utters through human agents. By that I mean that the *Bath Qol* events, the voice that Jesus heard from heaven on different occasions (at his baptism, and transfiguration, Mk. 1:11 and 9:7, and before his passion, Jn. 12:28), do not belong here; they may indeed qualify as word of God, but they had no future in the ongoing theology of the word. It is different with the concepts of prophecy, of inspiration, and of the efficacy they derive from the fact that God is active in his word; these we must study in their significance for history.

Dodd distinguishes two stages of prophecy in the Old Testament; in one the prophet speaks in something like a trance, in the other he is in more tranquil possession of his message. The first is prominent in earlier times and is related to practices in other religions whose "men of God" partake of the uncanny. Sometimes this is due to a mysterious personal endowment: There is a seer, speaking in a trance; or he is "possessed," with the "strong breath" of God upon him. In the Hebrew language he was called *nabi*, translated as prophet but applied to men who, with the exception of such outstanding figures as Samuel and Nathan, were often less like a prophet than like the modern dervish. With the great prophets of later times we come to the second stage. Now, while violent "seizure" by the Spirit is not wholly eliminated, the prophet is not characterized by such phenomena, but rather by the rational possession and utterance of his message. Sometimes, indeed, the great prophets repudiate the very name of *nabi* (Amos 7:14), or criticize the class and distinguish their own gift from that of such ecstatic performers (Jer. 23:38ff.).[21]

In the New Testament it is standard doctrine that God spoke through the prophets of the Old Testament, and it is largely taken for granted that the prophet was in rational possession of his mind and speech. But the early church experienced troubles of her own with the ecstatic type of performer. It was not denied that the Holy Spirit was active here as elsewhere. As Paul himself never doubted that he worked in the power of the Holy Spirit when he evangelized (1 Thess. 1:5; 1 Cor. 2:4; Rom. 15:18-19; etc.), and as no believer could "say 'Jesus is Lord!' except under the influence of the Holy Spirit" (1 Cor. 12:3), so "the gift of ecstatic utterance" is "the work of one and the same Spirit" (1 Cor. 12:10-11). But Paul "would rather speak five intelligible words . . . than thousands . . . in the language of ecstasy" (1 Cor. 14:19). So prophecy ranked high in the complex hierarchy of "offices" in the church:

> For Paul, prophecy was one of God's greatest gifts to his church for edification . . . and he ranked the prophet second only to an apostle in honor and importance. . . . By "prophecy," Paul understands intelligible preaching that builds up the church in faith . . . explains mysteries, and imparts knowledge.[22]

Paul does not seem to equate such prophecy with speaking the word of God, but it is a gift of the Spirit (1 Cor. 12:10, 28; 13:2), and his own utterances of this type are "in words found . . . not by . . . human wisdom but by the Spirit" (1 Cor. 2:13).

This early veneration for prophets in the church was not maintained: "The ministry of prophets exhibited a noticeable decline in effectiveness in the postapostolic age."[23] Possibly the rise of false prophets contributed to their being phased out; there are warnings against them already in Mark (13:22), and the danger seems to have grown greater at a later time (see 1 Jn. 4:1; Apoc. 16:13; 19:20; 20:10). Further, the institutional church would tend to replace the individual in the exercise of the various offices; thus, even though there is an extraordinary development of the doctrine of the Spirit in Luke, the tendency seems to be toward the role of the Spirit in the church: It is to officially appointed witnesses that the Spirit first comes on Pentecost, and the "council" that met at Jerusalem had the assistance of the Spirit in drawing up its decree. Even in John the trend is away from special charisms for particular people; the accent is on the gift that is made to all alike: "The initiation which you received from him stays with you; you need no other teacher" (1 Jn. 2:27).

Besides prophecy there is inspiration, though it is a Cinderella in comparison. From the viewpoint of God's action and his use of men as his instruments, there is no reason why inspiration should take second rank to prophecy, but then we do not generally view the universe from that perspective. So the relative spontaneity of the spoken word, the rapidity of its articulation, the immediacy of the link between inner emotion and linguistic expression, all of these surely were factors in attributing divine influence to those who spoke of God and for God. Writing, on the contrary, slows one down; the rational takes over; and it is not so apparent that God is at work in the written production. At any rate in the Old Testament the inspiration of the scriptures as such just begins to be hinted at in the command God gives the prophet to write his word (Ex. 17:14; 34:27; Is. 8:1; Jer. 36:1ff.). Even in the New Testament, with its high regard for the scriptures, there is little on inspiration.

However, the doctrine does surface in the New Testament, just in time to offset the decline in charismatic leadership in the living church, and with momentous consequences for the theology of the word. Two texts, both late, were responsible for the development. One of them occurs in the Pastorals and uses the fateful word itself, *theopneustos*. The author has been recommending the sacred writings to Timothy, and continues: "Every inspired scripture has its use for teaching and truth and refuting error, or for reformation of manners and discipline in right living" (2 Tim. 3:16). While the English word "inspired" retains the link with *spirit* that *theopneustos* has with *pneuma*, it omits the reference to the divine. Literally, we should translate "breathed by God"; then the Old Testament origins of the idea show up more clearly: "The word is doubtless intended to suggest that God has breathed life-giving truth into the scriptures just as he breathed into man's nostrils the breath of life and man became a living soul."[24] The second text, in the very late letter, 2 Peter, gives this doctrine a sharper focus, linking the scriptures with prophecy and minimizing the human role. The author, after recommending attention to the prophets, says: "But first note this: no one can interpret any prophecy of Scripture by himself. For it was not through any human whim that men prophesied of old; men they were, but, impelled by the Holy Spirit, they spoke the words of God" (2 Pet. 1:20-21).

Richardson finds that the biblical concept of inspiration that emerges in the Pastorals "bears little relation to the later notion of inspiration which became Hellenized in the early centuries and led to the view that the Heb. prophets and Christian Apostles were inspired after the manner of Vergil's Sibyl."[25] This may be, and the fact that Jewish thought took a similar turn in Philo, who spoke of the Spirit using the inspired writer as a flute,[26] supports the view of a Hellenizing influence. But perhaps the matter is not quite so simple. The circumstances were right, independently of the Hellenizers. We have to remember that, in becoming a Christian book, the Old Testament was read much more as a prophecy of future events than had been the case before. In the Old Testament role of the prophets as interpreters of history there was not the same need to emphasize their inspiration; but when they are understood to foretell the gospel it is natural to underline the influence of the Holy Spirit. This is clear already in 1 Peter:

> This salvation was the theme which the prophets pondered and explored, those who prophesied about the grace of God awaiting you. They tried to find out what was the time, and what the circumstances, to which the spirit of Christ in them pointed, foretelling the sufferings in store for Christ and the splendours to follow; and it was disclosed to them that the matter they treated of was not for their time but for yours (1:10-12).

Whatever the causes, the theme introduced by 2 Timothy and 2 Peter was taken up by the early ecclesiastical writers. Athenagoras seems to have been among the first of the Christians to employ the figure of the musical instrument: The Spirit uses the prophets "as a flautist might play upon his flute,"[27] but all the apologists emphasized the "miraculous, inspired perfection of the Old Testament."[28] And Campenhausen traces the concept of inspiration through Justin (again for the Old Testament), Theophilus of Antioch (for the gospels), Ireneus (more tentatively in him), and (in a somewhat diluted form) Clement of Alexandria, to find that "Tertullian makes a start on a formal, thought out concept of inspiration for the whole Bible." However, it is Origen who is the real theologian of inspiration. He goes far beyond Tertullian's

> sober lawyer's reflections, and in particular, he develops the idea not simply on an *ad hoc* basis, in order to extract the truth he wants from a particular text, but in principle, as an established article of belief. . . . Origen is thus a champion of verbal inspiration, and in principle hardly less strictly so than his Jewish contemporaries, with whom he was also associated. Consequently his whole exegetical technique is bound up with the single word, and indeed never balks even at finding a meaning "in the most accidental letters."[29]

A third heading is the efficacy of the word. Its doctrinal course was quite different from that of inspiration. Where the latter would grow and flourish, the former would go into a long decline, to experience a rejuvenation only in post-scholastic times. This decline is surely linked with that so-called Western concentration on truth which we will be studying in our next chapter. The next swing of the pendulum will bring back the notion of efficacy with the modern emphasis on the word as an encounter with God, but that is a long way off in history; our present concern is simply to notice an attribute of the word that was displaced to the margins of thought in the course of the centuries.

It is difficult for those trained in the analytic, scientific manner of thinking to enter into the Hebrew mind and grasp that special dynamic character of the word we are dealing with now. However, the literature on the point is emphatic and helps us over the hurdles. The Hebrew *dabar*, we are told, does indeed mean "a spoken utterance of any kind, a saying, a speech, narrative, message, command, request, promise, etc.," as is the case in the West. But it also means more than that: It means "a matter, affair, event, act, etc." Further:

> It was the common belief in ancient times that words, once uttered, had a strange inherent power of their own, especially words of blessing or cursing, cf. Isaac's blessing of Jacob, which once given could not be recalled (Gen. 27). The words of the Lord always had the power appropriate to their particular character, and were effective for their particular purpose; cf. Isa. 55.11, "so shall my word be that goeth forth out of my mouth: it shall not return unto me void, but it shall accomplish that which I please, and it shall prosper in the thing whereto I sent it."[30]

All these qualities are carried forward into New Testament thinking on the word. There too it is a spoken utterance. And it is something that happens: "Come, we must go straight to Bethlehem and see this thing (*rêma*) that has happened" (Lk. 2:15; see Acts 10:37). But it also had the active, efficacious aspect that is our present topic.

This efficacity is affirmed in the very text that we found to be of such central importance: "When we handed on God's message, you received it, not as the word of men, but as what it truly is, the very word of God *at work in you* who hold the faith" (1 Thess. 2:13). It is the character that the evangelists attribute to the healing word of Jesus: "He speaks with authority. When he gives orders, even the unclean spirits submit" (Mk. 1:27). "But the centurion replied. . . . You need only say the word and the boy will be cured" (Mt. 8:8). The same character appears in Acts, not only in the effective word of the apostles, but in the personified word that grows and becomes strong and spreads widely (6:7; 12:24; 13:49; 19:20; and see 2 Thess. 3:1). But this personification remains subordinate to the idea that it is God who is at work in the word and is responsible for its power. That is why we pray that the word may prosper: "Pray for us, that the word of the Lord may have everywhere the swift and glorious course that it has had among you" (2 Thess. 3:1). Paul goes so far as to identify the word with the power of God: "This doctrine (*logos*) of the cross is sheer folly to those on their way to ruin, but to us who are on the way to salvation it is the power of God" (1 Cor. 1:18).

The effects of the word can be specified. First, there is a series of adjectival phrases where the genitive may be objective or subjective but in either case suggests what is accomplished: the word of life (Phil. 2:16), the word of salvation (Acts 13:26), the word of his grace (Acts 14:3; 20:32), etc. Further, there are passages that link word and sacrament in efficacy: "Of his set purpose, by declaring the truth, he gave us birth" (Jas. 1:18); "You have been born anew, not of mortal parentage but of immortal, through the living and enduring word of God" (1 Pet. 1:23; see also Eph. 5:26; 1 Tim. 4:4-5; Jn. 15:3; 17:17-19). And there is continuity with the Old Testament doctrine of the creative word: "There were heavens and earth long ago, created by God's word. . . . And the present heavens and earth, again by God's word, have been kept in store for burning" (2 Pet. 3:5-7). Hebrews asserts the same doctrine as 2 Peter, but from a more cheerful perspective: ".The Son . . . sustains the universe by his word of power" (1:3).

Kittel points out that the efficacy of the word is not to be understood as some form of magic:

> The efficacy of the Word is dependent on its Author, but is also assured by His will. . . . It increases through His power. . . . The Word has within it the effective *charis* of the One who has spoken it. . . .
>
> Not in itself as a magical entity, but as the Word of God, i.e., the Word spoken and used by God, the Word is efficacious. . . . This is also implied in the common image of the weapon.[31]

The reference here is to the two-edged sword of Hebrews: "For the word of God is alive and active. It cuts more keenly than any two-edged sword, piercing as far as the place where life and spirit, joints and marrow, divide" (4:12).

This efficacy of the word gives a new character to human response. Of course, the general features, briefly indicated in chapter one, of response to the message are still operative: The word encounters us, it calls us to hear, obey, decide, and act. But there is now another feature to be brought into focus, and Kittel serves to introduce it, as he expresses a view that is especially congenial to Protestant thinking. There is, he says in regard to the word, a dialectic of grasping and being grasped, but it is the latter that is primary: "At the beginning of every relation of man to the Word stands the passive." This does not require that the other side of the coin be forgotten: "The Word must be received and maintained. This means that it can be accepted or rejected." The regular word for accepting it is *dechesthai*, but the sense is specified by the Hebrew meaning of *akouein*, to hear (with a good heart), and of *pisteuein*, to believe (and adhere to). Finally, the word is truly heard when it is done: "Only be sure that you act on the message and do not merely listen; for that would be to mislead yourselves" (Jas. 1:22).[32]

This doctrine that the message is the word of God and that God is active in its utterance and in its commitment to writing will give direction to our history as we move forward. It is not without its unhappy side. The eternal character of the word will be overstated. The individuality of the human author will be overlooked; after all, can it matter whether Paul or Jude or John wrote the word, when God is the main author? The hierarchy of truths will be confused; is it not equally the word of God when we read that the Word became flesh and that Paul left his cloak at Troas? And this unhappy side will be brought even more into view with the shift to the theme of truth that we are to study as the next stage in our history.

CHAPTER THREE

THE WORD OF GOD AS TRUTH

Two centuries after its beginnings the Christian message, now handed down and accessible primarily in the scriptures of Old and New Testaments, is firmly established as the word of God, and the sacred writers are universally conceived to have written under the inspiration of the Holy Spirit, just as the prophets are conceived to have spoken under his influence. That is the net result of the previous chapter, and on this basis we ask: What is the direction of the next step? Is it possible to find a theme that focuses the ongoing theology of the word at this point and will provide a context for the themes that will emerge later in history?

The range of possibilities is great, for, though "word" is one aspect of a richer reality, it is still itself a many-splendored thing and can be considered from many angles. We can consider it linguistically, and then we are in the field of philology. We can consider it as the expression of those who wrote it or spoke it, individualists often to a high degree, and then we exercise the romantic type of hermeneutic that relies strongly on empathy. We can consider it as an encounter with the living God, and then we are challenged personally to conversion and a new way of life. We can consider it as the source of many diverse encounters, and then we study it in relation to various traditions, doctrines, theological systems. We can consider it not only as an event in itself, but also as a narrative of events, and then we have the course of that narrated history to occupy us. We can consider it as the expression of a mentality quite different from our own, and then we have the task of exegesis, to explain in terms more adapted to our understanding what really is being said. Finally, as just one possibility among many, we have the aspect of truth that cannot be contradicted, and then we study it as the source of the articles of faith that we profess and the doctrines that we hold.[1]

43

It is this last aspect that seems to focus the ongoing theology of the word at this time and prolong the trajectory that will bring us to the further stages in its history. So we can summarize the sequence of these three chapters by saying that in the beginning was the good news, and the good news was thematized as the word of God, and the word of God was thematized as truth.

No doubt, this transition was expedited once the work of theology was taken over by the Greek-trained minds of the Western world. But I would urge a degree of critical sobriety here. There is a dynamism of mind that is neither Eastern nor Western, but pertains simply to the spontaneity of the human spirit as such. Ideas arise in the Hebrew mind as they do in the Greek; they are as prone to error in the one as in the other, and demand in both cases the verifying procedures of the critical approach (more of this presently). Furthermore, the very fact that the operative thinking of the church occurred in Western minds using Western categories, while the main sources of the message remained Eastern, called forth a mode of conceiving and communicating the message that could migrate across cultural boundaries, and this was provided in the truths that emerged in the following centuries, truths whose import was universal and "catholic," even though the language was Greek.[2]

One more thing should be explained by way of introduction: our use of the word "truth" in this chapter. Our meaning, then, is the plain and simple one that we intend when we speak of "the true state of affairs," or that we translate into other words when we say that we want "to get at the facts." It is what we seek when we ask a question whose answer is yes or no. For example: Is the Son God in the same sense as the Father is God? With such a question we are dealing with truth, whether we use the term or not, and, when we search the word of God to find the answer, we have thematized the word as truth.[3]

The reader will recognize my example as the question that the council of Nicea answered in the year 325 with a peremptory yes. I chose the example advisedly. In fact, the new phase of history we are entering in this chapter is the conciliar phase. It was in the councils, with their stock censures—"If anyone say . . . let him be anathema"—that truth emerged most clearly as a theme. Like the emergence of the idea that the Christian message is the word of God, this was an event; it happened in the concrete universe of space and time. That is not to say that it happened suddenly in one giant leap. On the contrary, there is a long history. There was a prior history going back to the earliest New Testament writings, and there was a subsequent history leading right up to the recent past. That is the sequence that I must now attempt to trace.

1. The Exercise of Truth in the Early Church

The question now, as we open the pages of the New Testament, is not primarily whether the message we read there is true or not. We might, of course, challenge John when he says that Jesus is the Christ, the Son of God, and ask him: Is that really true? Such a question would be a second moment in our study, but it is not the main objective. The main question is whether truth in the sense defined is a concern of John at all, not whether he was right or wrong in what he said.

The answer to this once seemed too obvious to bother about; nothing is easier than to run through the New Testament, and especially John, collecting occurrences of the word *alêtheia* (and its cognates) which the translations render by "truth." However, biblical scholarship has taught us that the matter is not so simple. In the Old Testament, we are told, "Truth means essentially reliability, dependableness, ability to perform what is required." And so the Hebrew words generally translated by "truth" are sometimes rendered by "faithfulness."[4] In the New Testament the word is found to have six meanings, each with a train of connotations: It means that which has certainty or force, or that on which one can rely, or the real state of affairs as disclosed, or the truth of statement; a fifth meaning is the true teaching or faith, with connotations of authority on one side and of obedience on the other; finally, it can mean genuineness, divine reality, revelation—a usage developing out of Hellenistic dualism and determining the highly individual terminology of John.[5]

To answer my question through a word-study of New Testament usage is therefore a task for scholars. If I am to be faithful to our program of specialization, I had best follow my usual route of attending more to what the writers do than to the thematic words they use. As before, the words of the New Testament remain the data. But now the words to be studied are not "true" and "false" and their cognates and associates; rather, it is the words that indicate the operations and intentions of these writers, that tell us what they are about. Specifically, the relevant data would be found in words like "is" and "yes" rather than in "true," and in "is not" and "no" rather than in "false." Such words reveal, or may reveal, the exercise of truth long before there is conceptualization of the notion.

A clue to this exercise is the explicit or implicit occurrence of questions for reflection. Questions on the cognitional level are of two kinds: There are questions for understanding that ask, What? How? Why? etc.; the response to them is an idea. There are also questions for reflection that ask: Is that so? and the response to them is yes or no or maybe. In the fully articulated original case, questions for understanding come first: There is data, which is material for inquiry and understanding; we strive to understand it, and the striving is equivalent to asking: What is it? Only when we have formed an idea, a possible explanation, do we go on to ask whether the idea is correct, the question for reflection.[6] However, the fully articulated case is not the everyday case. Rarely in adult life do we deal with a pure original case, for we come to the inquiry with a set of concepts that express our habitual understanding and eliminate the need of questions for understanding. So this chapter deals mainly with questions for reflection; questions for understanding are a marginal factor in the second section, where they are needed to put Bauer's work in proper perspective, but they will be central only in chapter five.

Questions for reflection occur, then, in scripture. They may be quite explicit: " 'Are you the one who is to come, or are we to expect some other?' " (Mt. 11:3). They may be explicit but in the mode of indirect discourse: "The people were on the tiptoe of expectation, all wondering about John, whether perhaps he was the Messiah" (Lk. 3:15). They may be revealed in the state of doubt and agitation that the subject experiences: "When they saw him, they fell prostrate before him, though some were doubtful" (Mt. 28:17). They may be merely implicit in the dialogue: "We are certain now that you know everything" (Jn.

16:30); that is, previously it had been a question to them. A very
good index of the question for reflection is the state of contradiction between two opponents, for the question always admits the
two answers, yes and no. A simple example is the story of the
two harlots arguing before Solomon (1 Kings 3:17ff.); there may
have been no question in the mind of the one who said, Yes, it is
my baby, and none in the mind of the other who said, No, it is
not, but they certainly posed a question for Solomon. A New
Testament example would be the division Jesus caused among
the Jews, some believing him to be the Messiah, others arguing
against it: "Thus he caused a split among the people" (Jn. 7:43).
Paul's long argument with those who denied the resurrection of
the dead is also a helpful example (1 Cor. 15:12ff.). For this
reason it greatly illuminates a writer's purpose and helps us determine what he is asserting as the truth, to know who it is he
opposes: Against whom was John writing? against whom was
Matthew writing? Even more clearly than the question for reflection, the contradiction shows that truth is the issue.

Under this heading belongs a great deal of data in the New
Testament on the opposite of truth: falsity and lying, error and
heresy, and the like. It is illuminating to collect the occurrences
of *planê* and its cognates (they occur more than fifty times), and
reflect on the concern they manifest in the early church about
"straying" from the truth. As for deceit and lying, 2 Peter applies
to the New Testament category of teachers what the Old Testament applied to prophets: "But Israel had false prophets as well
as true; and you likewise will have false teachers among you"
(2:1). The author goes on to say: "They will import disastrous
heresies, disowning the very Master who bought them." Here we
have a word, heresy, that originally referred simply to a choice
and came to designate a party, but now is veering toward its
modern meaning (see also Tit. 3:10). A similar history attaches
to the use of *heteros* and *allos*, used adjectivally to denote doctrines that depart from those handed down.[7]

However, I am myself straying from my purpose now,
which was not to conduct a word-study but to observe perfor-
mances. Let me then draw attention to Paul's performance in
dealing with opponents of his gospel: "If anyone preaches a
gospel at variance with the gospel which you received, let him be

outcast" (Gal. 1:9). The word "outcast" is more famous in the original (*anathema* in the Greek); it is not used against those who deny the resurrection, but the consequences are just as fatal: "If there be no resurrection, then Christ was not raised; and if Christ was not raised, then our gospel is null and void, and so is your faith; and we turn out to be lying witnesses for God" (1 Cor. 15:13-15). The Pastoral Letters reveal a similar performance, though against an opposite heresy; the teaching of those who propagate it is compared to infection that "will spread like a gangrene. Such are Hymenaeus and Philetus; they have shot wide of the truth in saying that our resurrection has already taken place, and are upsetting people's faith" (2 Tim. 2:17-18). In such procedures we see the same dynamism of the believing mind concerned to declare the true state of affairs against opponents. In all of them we notice the same supposition: Truth, in the sense of factual, assertory statement, is part of the word of God and the Christian message, and it utterly excludes its contradictory.

I would agree that to single out truth in the scriptures and separate it from the pastoral content in which it occurs is artificial. Clearly the New Testament writers do not thematize truth simply for its own sake; if I thought they did, I would not locate that step in the conciliar period. John is a good illustration of the way truth subserves a further purpose; he wrote his gospel, not only that we might believe "that Jesus is the Christ, the Son of God," but also that through this faith we might "possess eternal life by his name" (20:31). Similarly, the error, the straying, the heresy against which the early church struggled was not simply an intellectual matter; consequently, the exhortation is regularly not addressed to the mind of the believer, rather is he urged to build on good foundations, to guard the deposit, to keep watch, to stand firm, and the like. Colossians offers a useful epitome of this attitude: "Only you must continue in your faith, firm on your foundations, never to be dislodged from the hope offered in the gospel" (1:23). This double concern is seen in the double use of certain verbs. Thus, *pisteuein* is used both for belief *in* and belief *that*: The disciples believed in Christ, adhering to him in trust (Jn. 2:11 and passim), but they also believed with Paul "that Jesus died and rose again" (1 Thess. 4:14). *Homologein* has a parallel two fold use: There is the act of confessing Christ before men, professing adherence to him (Mt. 10:32), but there is also the confession "Jesus is Lord" (Rom. 10:9).[8]

2. Truth Emerging As a Separate Concern

Between the scriptures and the first great council the trend toward a focus on the truth of the message continues. Thus Ignatius of Antioch shows a mentality very much like that of the New Testament, especially of John and the Pastoral Letters with which he may have been contemporaneous. His concern is illustrated in the following passage: "Stop your ears therefore when anyone speaks to you that stands apart from Jesus Christ . . . who was really born and ate and drank, really persecuted by Pontius Pilate, really crucified and died."[9] Again: "I merely wish to warn you betimes not to yield to the bait of false doctrine, but to believe most steadfastly in the birth, the Passion, and the Resurrection, which took place during the procuratorship of Pontius Pilate. Facts these are, real and established by Jesus Christ."[10] Polycarp would agree: "Therefore let us leave untouched the senseless speculations of the masses and the false doctrines, and turn to the teaching delivered to us in the beginning."[11] Papias, tied to the whipping-post by critics of tradition, is at least a witness to the concern for truth: "I shall not hesitate to set down . . . all the information I have ever carefully gathered from the presbyters. I carefully committed it to memory and vouch for its truth."[12] There is continuity in this right up to Ireneus and his rule of faith; this rule, he writes, exhorts us "to remember that we have received baptism for remission of sins, in the name of God the Father, and in the name of Jesus Christ the Son of God, who became incarnate and died and was raised, and in the Holy Spirit of God."[13]

The trend here is too slow to occupy us, for our business is change, not continuity, and we are looking for significant transitions in the emergence of the truth-function. However, there is one preliminary problem that was raised by Walter Bauer in his work on orthodoxy and heresy in the early church. We have proceeded as if truth were the given element, with heresy arising as a sort of perverse refusal to hear and obey a word that is plainly spoken with a definite message. Is that assumption justified? Have we not simply taken for granted a position that turns out under critical examination to be untenable? It would be Bauer's thesis that we have. The standard view, he says, already prevalent in the 2nd century, is that Jesus revealed the pure doctrine to his apostles who carried it round the world, that the devil then succeeded in sowing weeds in the divine wheat field, and that many Christians, blinded by him, abandoned the true doctrine; the sequence, then, is such that orthodoxy is first and heresy follows, not the other way around. Origen makes it explicit: "All heretics at first are believers; then later they swerve from the rule of faith."[14] Bauer's own position is almost exactly the opposite of Origen's: Heresy is not a corruption of an original orthodox faith, but in the beginning heresy and orthodoxy are not sharply divided; in fact, it is heresy rather than orthodoxy that is first on the scene. The trouble is, we have depended too much for our history of the matter on the vote of one party that happened to gain power and brand the opposition as heretical.[15]

Bauer's work forces us to a refinement of our account of the way truth emerges in the rational exercise of our minds. That exercise, we recall, depended on the occurrence of questions. Sometimes there is a stated proposition whose meaning is sufficiently clear, and then the question is one for reflection: Is it true? But sometimes no statement is proposed, there is not yet a question for reflection, and then the emergence of truth depends on the occurrence of the prior question for understanding and the ideas that provide a possible answer. Now the ideas may be right, but much more likely they will be wrong, simply because many explanations of the data are generally possible, but generally only one is correct. To apply this now to the Christian message: Along with the actual truth in the original kerygma, "the facts about Jesus," there is an enormous range of possibilities; there is an amorphous mass that is neither true nor false, but just data for inquiry and reflection. In Lonergan's terms, it has not yet been "promoted" to the level of truth.[16] Truth is achieved; you reach it by climbing to a new level. Even the word of God may not be true, not in the sense that it is false, but in the sense that it is neither true nor false; it may contain historical experience, ideas, hypotheses, and arguments, it may go on to exhort or rebuke, it may deal in various ways with words and deeds, all without bringing the matter to the critical issue of truth. Bauer's work, I believe, is to be read in the clarifying light of this analysis. At any rate this perspective will guide our own discussion of what happened in the conciliar phase of the theology of the word.

The immediate precursor of the conciliar mentality on truth is the credal form, which mediates between the scriptural confession of Christ and the definition of truth under pain of anathema. The original elements in the creed were scriptural, found in such statements as were "confessed" ("Jesus is Lord") or in such narratives of fact as were handed on ("I handed on to you the facts which had been imparted to me"). These early Christological confessions were complemented a generation later by the formula in Matthew which we have come to call trinitarian: "Baptize men everywhere in the name of the Father and the Son and the Holy Spirit" (28:19).

However, there is a century of obscurity between these scriptural elements and the creeds that clearly presage the conciliar definition. At one time it was an accepted tradition in the West that the twelve apostles, just before their dispersal to the four winds of the great mission-field, gathered for a last meeting and composed their creed, each apostle in turn contributing an article. The legend, propagated by Rufinus in the 5th century, was never an Eastern tradition; in fact, the bishops of the Orthodox Eastern church refused at the time of the council of Florence to have this Western "Apostles'" creed foisted upon them.[17] The attack became general in Renaissance times, and in 1443 the humanist scholar Valla was brought before the Inquisition for denying the ancient tradition. But it was only in 1647 that a definitive positive step forward was taken, with the discovery by James Ussher, bishop of Armagh, of a text that obviously antedated the one explained by Rufinus. And it was only from the 19th century on, with the work of Caspari, Harnack, Kattenbusch, Burn, and other more recent writers, that we have been able to trace the main steps in the development of the creed.[18]

They are roughly as follows. A century after Matthew we find in Ireneus a rule of faith, in the sense of a rule prescribed by faith; this is close to a creed but not yet the later category. In

Tertullian there is more definite use of a credal form, identified with the rule of faith adopted in Rome and Africa, and used as a *tessera*, a token. This metaphor is taken from a custom of hospitality: There was "an earthenware token, which two friends divided and passed on to their descendants, making the duty of friendship hereditary." At this time, therefore, the creed may have become a badge of Christian profession, admitting the Christian to social meals in churches where he was a stranger. That seems to be the idea also in the use of the term *symbolum* among Christians. *Symbolum* became technical, if not in Tertullian, then certainly in Cyprian, for whom it meant the short creed put in interrogative form to candidates at baptism, a form that endures even in our own day. From such beginnings, the "Apostles' " creed developed, and also, presumably, the creed that was employed as the basis of the first conciliar definition at Nicea in 325.[19]

The sequence is from a word of confession in which there is truth-content, to a creed that selects the truth-content for special attention and makes it a password, to a conciliar definition that sets two contradictory statements in opposition, choosing one as an article of faith and condemning the other as heretical. I would certainly not say that the sequence occurs without overlapping, but the emphasis in scripture does seem to be on confessing Christ, the creeds do seem to become an admission requirement, and in the councils we do find what amounts to a formal process of fixing and imposing the truth and anathematizing the contrary.

3. Nicea: Truth in the Spotlight

At Nicea we finally have, for the first time, the formal definition of an article of faith by an ecumenical council, and the beginning of a long period, lasting for hundreds of years, in which there would be a concentration on the truth contained in the word of God. The hundreds of years pertain to the routine and the repetitive, and are not the stuff from which history is made. But Nicea marks the transition and it is important to see what was going forward in that council. From the viewpoint of many critics, the salient feature seems to be the Hellenizing of dogma, but from our viewpoint the salient is the emergence and differentiation of the truth-function of the word.

It *is* the word of God that provides the context in which discussion took place. This was not as explicit as I am making it, but it was the supposition; everyone involved in the controversy, whether he appealed to the tradition of his local church, or quoted earlier writers of blessed memory, or argued directly from the scriptures, or even used philosophical principles, knew that the ultimate source that must justify his position was what God had said. Next, it was the truth in the word of God that was singled out, round which the battle raged. Many diverse factors got entangled in the history, address and encounter, witness and fidelity, politics and piety, the clash of schools and personalities; but there is no doubt whatever about the key and central issue: What is the truth about the Son of God? It appears in the thrust of the Arian arguments; it appears more compactly in the way the Nicene fathers nailed down an article of faith on the question. First, they made positive additions to the creed that had been adopted as basis for their declaration: The Son is begotten from the Father, that is, from the substance of the Father; he is God from God, that is, true God from true God. They repeat: He is begotten, that is, not made; he is of one substance with the Father. Not satisfied with this, they turn to explicit condemnation of any who say the opposite, and they attach anathemas: Those who say that there was when he was not, or that before he was begotten he was not, or that he was made from (the world of) non-beings . . . these the Catholic church puts under anathema.[20]

This is not the language of prayer, though that of the creed into which the insertions were made presumably was. Much less is it the joyful proclamation of the good news, as the scriptural phrases at the core of that creed originally were. It is more like the language of a legal decision handed down by supreme court judges who wish to settle the matter in the most precise manner possible, eliminating every ambiguity and closing every loophole. It is the language that results when the truth of the kerygma is set forth as dogma, to be accepted by all who profess the Catholic faith, language suited to those articles of faith declared by the church. The first Vatican council will impose for belief those articles of faith that are contained in the word of God and are proposed by the church as divinely revealed and to be believed.[21]

What were the conditions under which such a differentiation

of the truth emerged from the context of living faith into such clear but solitary splendor? First, there was a definite question; we can formulate it now with greater simplicity as the question, Is the Son God in the same sense as the Father is God?[22] That modern formulation is a shorthand, but quite accurate, account of a real question that was really debated with considerable passion prior to and, to some extent, during the council. Next, since it has the form of a question for reflection, it admits of two answers: We may say yes, and we may say no. Third, Arius had answered no and, since his answer seemed to run counter to the faith and tradition of the church, the bishops of Nicea felt compelled, with a consensus amounting almost to unanimity, to answer yes.

That is a schematic account written today of what was going forward then. It does not imply that the Nicene bishops formulated in their own minds what they were doing from the viewpoint of ongoing theology. As Lonergan says, explaining the functional specialty of history, "in most cases, contemporaries do not know what is going forward."[23] A second point: Besides schematizing the ideas, I have telescoped the temporal duration. The question did not arise suddenly three centuries after Easter. On the contrary, it had taken a century and a half for it to reach the clarity it had at Nicea, and it would take another half century to achieve the clarification that would make Nicea acceptable. The question was inevitable from the time around A.D. 180 when believers began to speak of Father, Son, and Holy Spirit, as a "threesome," a *trias* or *trinitas*, for then they were putting Son and Spirit into a "class" with the Father. But the minds of believers, like those of all flesh-and-blood subjects thinking in concrete circumstances, move with a sluggishness far removed from the rapid clicking of a logic-machine. Before the question for reflection could be put in definite terms, the prior questions for understanding had to occur along with the ideas that would provide possible answers. There had been the wildly speculative ideas of the gnostics and the crudely naive answers of the adoptianists, but the possibility of a carefully elaborated orthodox answer rested in the dialectic running through Tertullian and Origen to end with the diametric opposition of Arius and the council.

The pattern set by Nicea has been followed in a long sequence of conciliar definitions reaching up to and including the first Vatican council. By and large the dogmatic issue has not changed; the chronicle is one of routine and repetition, without particular interest for history.[24] But there is a bit of history in regard to that formative work of theological thought which preceded Nicea as it must precede all properly defined articles of faith; it deserves a mention here, though we are dealing with what the theologians of the Greek Orthodox church call *theologoumena*, and not with articles of faith.

The history goes back to Origen who in that early period had already noted the distinction between articles of faith and theological opinions, as we would now name the two classes of doctrine. We have, he says, a definite rule in regard to some doctrines, but the apostles left other matters undefined, "their intention undoubtedly being to supply the more diligent of those who came after them . . . with an exercise on which to display the fruit of their ability."[25] Origen himself, and a rather steady stream of followers, have exercised the recommended diligence with great alacrity, sometimes with unhappy results and to the alarm of believers. Augustine would represent a certain focusing of Origen's point: He is one of the first to introduce the word "question" into his titles. At least eight of his works, as listed in the Migne edition, show this word in the title, and his preface to *Seven Books of Questions on the Heptateuch* reveals that he has thought a bit about the function of the question. He does not regard his questions as fully solved by his treatment of them; rather, he has supplied a memo on what remains to be done. He begs the reader not to consider it useless to propose questions without answers, "for it is part of successful discovery to know what you are looking for."[26]

Augustine does not focus especially on the question for reflection. Abelard comes much closer to doing just that, though he could not put it in those words, in his classic *Sic et non*. It is a collection of citations, mainly patristic but occasionally scriptural, in which Abelard deliberately sets opinion against opinion; his purpose is not to discredit authority (each author is an "authority") but to encourage thinking on the apparent contradiction, and thus contribute toward a solution of the difficulty:

"We begin to inquire when a doubt is raised, and by inquiry we arrive at the truth."[27] *Sic et non* was a forerunner for the *Sentences* of Peter Lombard later in the same century ("sententiae" meant opinions, and the opinions were often contradictory), and Peter in turn was a source for Thomas Aquinas, who regularly proceeded in four steps to state the question, give two contradictory answers, and provide his own solution. The pattern is familiar: There is a question whether. . . . The answer seems to be no, for. . . . But against that we read. . . . So to solve the question it must be said. . . .

In modern times there developed the notion of the theological "censure," that is, the characterization of a proposition in theology according to its binding force: Is it to be held in faith? Is it at least firmly probable? Or is it just the opinion of certain authors? Etc., etc. These censures belong to the era of the theology manuals, where the material is divided into theses, the precise question at issue is specified, the opposing opinions are listed, the answer is given in carefully defined terms and is proved by appeal to the sources. It is the thematization of truth brought to its ultimate stage, and pointing to a further thematization, the question of the *loci* of truth that will occupy us in chapter four.

The loss and gain involved in the thematizing of the Christian word as truth have been widely if not very satisfactorily debated. It is not the purpose of this book to evaluate history in the way that debate has proposed to do, but I may be allowed a paragraph here that goes deliberately beyond a factual account. It will, I think, contribute to an understanding of what was going forward and help justify, if not the actual event in history, at least the attention I have given it in this chapter.

Let me admit then that concentration on the truth can seem today to have been a very retrograde step indeed; the joy and dynamism of a word that is "alive and active" and "cuts more keenly than any two-edged sword" (Heb. 4:12) seems reduced to the cold and lifeless abstraction of a mere proposition. We might compare it to the joyless greeting a child receives when he runs triumphantly home from school, waving his prize and shouting his success before he is in the door, only to be met with the remark, "I'd better telephone the teacher and check on that; we don't want any mistakes in these matters." Yet this is surely not an accurate picture of what happened at Nicea. For our need of the truth is also part of our experience and, when we are in doubt and sore perplexed, as the church was in the fourth century, the need can be very great indeed. Then the truth-function of the church and her ability to settle as a great community what the individual cannot settle by his own resources can be good news too along with the dogma that results from it. The real problem after Nicea, I believe, was not the differentiation of truth but the integration of truth again into the full life of the believing community. This we should do and not leave the other undone.

CHAPTER FOUR

TRUTH AS GROUNDED IN SOURCES: THE QUESTION OF *LOCI*

What is the fourth stage in the ongoing theology of the Christian message? If one looks simply at the extent of the materials to be surveyed after Nicea and attempts to find a pattern and direction, some thematization that takes over to dominate progress in thinking, one may despair of organizing such a massive mountain of data; the ideas, movements, and documents seem to proliferate as we move forward in time. But, on the other hand, it may be that the trajectory grows clearer, that we can anticipate the direction of the next transition by asking what the antecedent probability is. That is, when truth has been established as a concern in the study of the Christian word, can we find a clue to the next concern by asking what is likely to follow truth in the sequence of ideas?

It seems to me that we may indeed hope by such a question to discover a clue, and I suggest that it will point to the "sources" of truth as the next thematization of the Christian word. That is, after truth comes the question of our grounds for asserting something as true. This is a normal sequence in daily life: If you tell a plain man something new, he is apt to ask: How do you know? It is the sequence in science: When a scientist forms an opinion on a question in his field, he is driven on to devise a crucial experiment that may settle the question on the basis of sufficient evidence. We can find a hint of this sequence in the instruction of 1 Peter: "Be always ready with your defence whenever you are called to account for the hope that is in you" (3:15). As a final preliminary, we might ask whether such a step is not latent in the procedures of the Nicene council that brought the previous chapter into focus; that is, was there not a feature of the Nicene debate that was not then the central theme but was very much a background factor in the movement of history at

58

that time, namely, the authority by which the council pronounced on Arius and defined the faith of the church?

This at any rate is the view I will propose in this chapter,
that, latent in the history of Nicea, there was the question once
put to Jesus: "By what authority are you acting like this? Who
gave you this authority?" (Mt. 21:23), and that this question will
later, very much later, become the theme that dominates the
theology of the Christian word. It will indeed require centuries
for the thematizing to occur; though it arises immediately in the
swift atemporal unfolding of logic, it is not till the 16th century
and the controversies between Lutherans and Roman Catholics
that historically the theme seems to come directly into focus, so
that one may say that the chronological leap from our third to
our fourth chapter is measured by the distance between Nicea
and Trent. Maybe we could choose a more definite symbol of the
new stage in Melchior Cano's *De locis theologicis*, a work published posthumously in the year 1563. From Nicea to the Reformation is a long interval, and the reader may wonder, as I did,
whether the next significant transition is not to be located in
some other emerging question; or, if it does lie in the question of
loci, whether that question did not come into focus before the
16th century. There are surely important anticipatory steps in
the long history between 325 and 1563, but it seems to me, after
pondering the evidence, that this thematization occurs in exact
form only at that later date. Let me set forth that evidence now
for the reader to examine.

1. New Testament Concern with Sources

In examining the New Testament we shall, as usual, give
more attention to the actual practices revealed there than to
conceptualizations of the idea of sources or *loci*. It is our familiar
concern with the *vécu* rather than with the *thématique*. Now the
earliest and most obviously relevant practice is that of using the
scriptures, that is, the Old Testament, to show the meaning and
validity of the Christian message about Jesus. I quote Dodd once
again:

> In its most summary form the *kerygma* consists of the an-
> nouncement of certain historical events in a setting which
> displays the significance of those events. The events in ques-

> tion are those of the appearance of Jesus in history . . . and
> the emergence of the Church. . . .
>   The significance attached to these events is mainly in-
> dicated by references to the Old Testament.[1]

Dodd speaks here of significance rather than of proof. We shall
return to that, but the point at the moment is that the scriptures,
now read as a Christian book, are a source book for the Christian
faith. This is a central fact in the history of the word. It could
hardly be otherwise, for the first Christians were Jews, cherish-
ing the faith of their fathers; if they were to accept God's new
revelation in his servant Jesus they had to see the life of Jesus as
consonant with what God had already taught them in his word,
for that word could not be set aside (Jn. 10:35). This was especially necessary when the facts about Jesus were so disconcerting, not to say scandalous. Thus Paul, in one of the earliest forms
of the kerygma, presents the death and resurrection of Jesus as
having happened "according to the scriptures" (1 Cor. 15:3, 4).
Thus too the recurring statements of Matthew: "All this happened in order to fulfil what the Lord declared through the
prophet" (1:22).

Various questions arise in regard to this fact: on the accuracy of Christian use of the Old Testament and the validity of the
exegesis performed;[2] on the sort of collection, if there was one,
the Christians made of Old Testament quotations;[3] on the creative genius who first read the Old Testament as a Christian book
and interpreted the events of Jesus' life by this means.[4] But from
my thematic viewpoint I am more interested in the mentality that
anticipates the question of *loci*, that is, in the arguments, proofs,
appeals to authority, that assume the need for grounding the
Christian truth in established sources.

As a preliminary, let us notice that the appeal to the
scriptures was conducted in the spirit of apologetic proof. Campenhausen is anxious to rescue Paul from such an unworthy
practice,[5] but Luke at least did not see anything shameful in
apologetics; on the contrary he shows Paul quite busy at it: "For
the next three Sabbaths he argued with them, quoting texts of
Scripture which he expounded and applied to show that the
Messiah had to suffer and rise from the dead" (Acts 17:2). The
Jews at Beroea are of the same mind as to procedures, for they

test the Christian arguments by recourse to the same authority: "The Jews here were more liberal-minded . . . they received the message with great eagerness, studying the scriptures every day to see whether it was as they [Paul and Silas] said" (Acts 17:11). Apollos is shown as following Paul's pattern: "He was indefatigable in confuting the Jews, demonstrating publicly from the scriptures that the Messiah is Jesus" (18:28). And, what must be most distressing if you dislike the notion of proof but accept Luke's account, the Lord Jesus "showed himself . . . after his death, and gave ample proof *(en pollois tekmériois)* that he was alive" (Acts 1:3).

But, besides Luke's testimony, there are the letters of Paul himself to illustrate his procedures. An example is found in the way he conducts the law-gospel debate, and I can make my point very simply by referring to Cerfaux's analysis of Galatians. In his division, the first part of the letter extends from 1:11 to 4:11; this part he calls apologetic and demonstrative. The first section, from 1:11 to 2:21, deals with the authority of Paul himself, and the second, from 3:1 to 4:11, with the solidity of Paul's doctrine. Cerfaux analyzes this second section as follows: There is a first proof of justification by faith, and it is based on the charismatic phenomena that followed the conversion of the Galatians (3:1-5). There is a second proof that is called scriptural, and it is based on familiar texts of the Old Testament (3:6-14). Third, the argument takes on a juridical cast as Paul compares law and covenant from the viewpoint of priority and authority (3:15-18). The rest of this first part of the letter is less to my purpose, but Cerfaux introduces the second, parenetic part (4:12 to 6:10) by saying that Paul, having completed the demonstration of his doctrine, can now speak to the hearts of the Galatians.[6]

This analysis of Galatians is extremely interesting: It does not merely illustrate Paul's practice of proving a doctrine from scripture; it also considerably widens the perspective. The apologetic and demonstrative part as a whole begins by dealing with Paul's credentials, and it proceeds by arguing from experiential and juridical bases as well as from scripture; in fact, the scriptural proof is a relatively short section of the letter. We shall return presently to the question of credentials, but at the moment I should like to move toward a more comprehensive basis on the question of sources. It is of some importance, I think, to seek a more comprehensive viewpoint here; otherwise the word of God gets locked in a compartment separated from the use of reason and then, with reason emerging as a factor, the unity of man is destroyed; he comes apart, with his religious and his secular thinking divided.

To begin with Paul, we may note that he can appeal to reason in support of an argument otherwise religiously based: "Does not Nature herself teach you that while flowing locks disgrace a man, they are a woman's glory?" (1 Cor. 11:13; see also Rom. 1:18-23 and 2:11-16). If people will not listen to reason he can call flatly on custom: "However, if you insist on arguing, let me tell you, there is no such custom among us, or in any of the congregations of God's people" (1 Cor. 11:16). He can give rulings of his own on marriage, and support them by argument from religious premises: "For the heathen husband now belongs to God through his Christian wife, and the heathen wife through her Christian husband. Otherwise your children would not belong to God, whereas in fact they do" (1 Cor. 7:14). The logical structure is significant; Paul is drawing a conclusion. But it is also significant that he draws his conclusions as a believer who has the help of God's Spirit: "That is my opinion," he says in regard to another ruling on marriage, "and I believe that I too have the Spirit of God" (1 Cor. 7:40).[7]

Similarly, the evangelists will show Jesus mingling reason and religious sources. He invokes, for example, the analogies of nature: "You can tell a tree by its fruit" (Mt. 12:33). He wonders that the intelligence operative in forecasting the weather is not applied to the signs of the times: "You know how to interpret the appearance of earth and sky; how is it you cannot interpret this fateful hour?" (Lk. 12:56). Besides such homely wisdom and religious common sense, there are arguments that require a more than ordinary theological skill, as when he goes beyond scripture to bring out its hidden implications: "Now about the resurrection of the dead, have you never read in the Book of Moses, in the story of the burning bush, how God spoke to him and said, 'I am the God of Abraham, the God of Isaac, and the God of Jacob'? God is not God of the dead but of the living" (Mk. 12:26-27). This is really worthy of the better theology manuals, and one can profit from throwing the argument into syllogistic form to compare the Lord's reasoning with that of later theology.

Let us return to the question of credentials referred to earlier. Recall first Dodd's summary view of early Christian theologizing as a preaching of certain saving facts that were invested with a religious significance through reference to the scriptures. Now in regard to both the facts and their interpretation the question of credentials comes up. We are moving from the objective message and its two fold aspect to the subject, the agent of the message. If he is going to give rulings on religious matters, as Paul did, or otherwise assume authority that belongs to prophet and leader, he needs credentials under that heading; but even if he simply narrates the facts, the same question comes up insofar as his hearers need assurance that, like the witness from heaven, he speaks of what he knows and testifies to what he has seen (Jn. 3:11). The notion of testing credentials would be familiar to the early church from Old Testament efforts to discern true prophets from false.[8] And sooner or later the question was bound to be raised about New Testament agents of the word as well.

It is time now to go back from the Christian word as we conceived it first, the message of Easter, to Jesus himself, his own teaching and preaching. We are not ready to discuss the content of his message, but it is convenient here to introduce the question of his authority, credentials being hardly the word to describe his claims to a hearing. Need I say that I am not settling any question whatever about the "historical" Jesus? The question is directly about the early church and how it understood the message and authority of Jesus. It may be misleading here even to speak of a question. The enemies of Jesus did question his authority but those who followed him with open hearts seemed beyond such challenges. For Paul, when there is a word of Jesus, the matter is ended, and he clearly distinguishes his own word from that of the Lord Jesus (1 Thess. 4:15; 1 Cor. 7:10, 12, 25). Besides the Lord's word there is the tradition of his deeds: "For the tradition which I handed on to you came to me from the Lord himself; that the Lord Jesus, on the night of his arrest, took bread . . ." (1 Cor. 11:23). And this is the way the evangelists will later present Jesus, as one whose words and deeds have unquestioned authority: "The people were astounded at his teaching, for, unlike the doctors of the law, he taught with a note of authority" (Mk. 1:22). "He speaks with authority. When he gives orders, even the unclean spirits submit" (Mk. 1:27). His way of life, and especially his way of death, are cited as having an authority equal to his words: "Christ suffered on your behalf, and thereby left you an example; it is for you to follow in his steps" (1 Pet. 2:21). Perhaps even more significant than such explicit statements is the whole tenor of the way he is presented as acting and teaching. It appears in the familiar, "Amen, amen, I say to you," and it appears in the total assurance with which he goes beyond the law of his fathers: "You have learned that our forefathers were told. . . . But what I tell you is this . . ." (Mt. 5:21-22).[9]

From Jesus we turn to the apostles, who also preach the word with power and conviction. Paul brought the gospel "not in mere words but in the power of the Holy Spirit" (1 Thess. 1:5). An addition to Mark's gospel says the Eleven "went out to make their proclamation everywhere, and the Lord worked with them and confirmed their words by the miracles that followed" (Mk. 16:20; see Acts 3:1-12; 5:15-16; etc.). But there are profound differences. The authority of Jesus seemed transparently visible in his very performance; whether it was in the power of his words or in the signs that accompanied them does not matter much. That is, he did not seem to bother, or to have to bother, with credentials. Not so the apostles; with them the question of credentials emerges, more passionately in Paul, more matter-of-factly in Luke's account in Acts.

Obviously, some concrete cause and occasion brought the matter to a head for Paul. In his first letter to the Thessalonians he does not make a great deal of his role as an apostle; but six years later, in his first letter to the Corinthians, it is a raging issue and, in his second letter to that church, Paul is close to being neurotic on the question. He feels obliged now to show his credentials, while resisting the demand for them (3:10) and begins bitterly, chafing under the necessity, to elaborate his apology. In a general way, he claims God as the source of his authority (3:5-6; 4:7); in particular, he refers to his conduct as recommending him (6:6-7), asserts that the "marks of a true apostle" were evident in his work (12:12), warns them that the proof they seek of Christ's speaking in him will be given in the severity he (Paul) will show (13:3), and—what seems to shame him most of all —resorts to his visions, "boasting" of them in order to counterbalance the claims of his opponents, "these superlative apostles" (12:11; 11:5), these "sham-apostles . . . masquerading as apostles of Christ" (11:13).

The details of Paul's struggle to be accepted do not concern me. The main point lies in its significance for the theology of the word: Whatever happened between 1 Thessalonians and 1 Corinthians, it brought starkly into view the need the agents of the word had for credentials. Of course, Paul was a special case, but the same need appeared in its own way for the original apostles; and, as happened before, it is once more Luke who focuses the question. The synoptic gospels in general anticipate the question when they invest the Twelve with authority just by calling them "twelve" and thus implying that they succeed to the role of the twelve tribes. Acts indicates the new phase by using "apostles" to replace the "Twelve": Where the gospels insist on the latter and only occasionally speak of apostles, Acts reverses the priority and speaks regularly of apostles. And yet the statistics of word-usage do not reveal the full impact of Luke's contribution; that appears rather in the new understanding he provides of an apostle's function. The apostle is specified in Acts as one who can "witness" in a special and privileged way to Jesus.

The term "witness" represents a significant new phase in the history of the Christian word and should not be too lightly associated with "gospel" and "preaching" as if the three belonged to the same period and revealed similar interests. Paul uses the word, true enough: "we bore witness that he raised Christ to life" (1 Cor. 15:15; and see 1:6; 2 Cor. 1:12; 2 Thess. 1:10); his usage may even have given Luke the needed impetus. But it still falls far short of the technical sense the word receives in Acts. Mark, we could say, invokes a series of witnesses to give testimony to Jesus; the Father (1:11; 9:7), the demons (3:11; 5:7), the centurion (15:39), all of them bear out the testimony Mark himself gave in the title of his gospel to Jesus as Son of God. However, Mark does not, in any of these cases, use the word witness (but see 13:9). It is Luke who makes the term technical. The end of his gospel introduces the theme: "It is you who are the witnesses to all this" (24:48). The beginning of Acts picks it up (1:8), and three significant passages clarify his use of the term. First, there is the choice of a successor for Judas; it must be someone, Peter enjoins, who was with them in the days of the Lord Jesus: "One of those must now join us as a witness to his resurrection" (1:21-22). Next comes a sermon in which Peter, after relating the facts about Jesus, says that God "allowed him to appear, not to the whole people, but to witnesses whom God had chosen in advance, to us, who ate and drank with him after he rose from the dead" (10:41). And, third, there is the commission given Paul to be a witness "to what you have seen and heard" (22:15; see 26:16).

Luke does not define the term rigorously, and the criterion he gives early in Acts is not rigidly followed. Matthias was chosen to be both apostle and witness; the two functions are not clearly distinguished at this point (Acts 1:22-26). Perhaps Luke means to reserve a special role for the eyewitnesses who had seen "the events that have happened among us" (Lk. 1:1), and to allow "witness" a wider extension. At any rate he loosens the requirement Peter had laid down and admits Stephen (Acts 22:20) along with Paul as witness. Further, the object to which witness is given is also loosened: It includes not only the facts about Jesus but "what you shall yet see of me" (26:16). We are not surprised, then, when in some late books of the New Testament the further sense appears of professing faith in Jesus, often with courage and sacrifice. Luke himself almost sanctions this use in his account of Stephen's witness (Acts 7 compared with 22:20); Hebrews does the same in reference to Old Testament witnesses to the faith (12:1), but most of all it is the Apocalypse that accomplishes the shift. Here Jesus himself is the faithful witness (1:5; 3:14; see 1 Tim. 6:13), there is reference to "the blood of those who had borne their testimony to Jesus" (17:6; see 11:3ff.), and a special feature of the book is the suffering that accompanies witnessing to Christ (6:9, 11; 11:7; 12:11, 17; 20:4). The way is being prepared for the modern sense of the term "martyr."

In John's letter and gospel there is an explosion in the use of the term. We might have expected this, given John's legal motif: the judicial process that runs through the encounters Jesus has with his adversaries and will continue when his disciples, fortified now with a new Advocate, undergo their own accusation and trial.[10] But the frequency with which witness and its cognate forms occur is altogether phenomenal. Not only that, but there is the same deepening of meaning that we found in regard to *logos*: We are carried beyond the boundaries of earth when Jesus appeals to the witness of his Father (5:31ff. and 8:13ff.); again, if we accept human testimony much more should we accept divine, and the threefold testimony of water, blood, and Spirit is that of God himself for his Son (1 Jn. 5:9ff.). But once more, as with the Johannine *logos*, this anticipates a later phase in the ongoing history of theology; it does not directly belong with the precise theme of this chapter.

Refinements are endless in study of the New Testament "witness," but I have tried to keep my eye on the main issue: Does the emerging use of this technical term indicate a new concern for the credentials of the agents of the word? and is it an unexamined assumption that puts "witness" in the same class historically with "gospel" and "kerygma"? If, despite errors of detail, the main lines of my argument are found acceptable, we have here an important element of ongoing history recorded within the confines of the New Testament itself. Many years have passed now since the Lord Jesus lived among his disciples. In chapter three we already saw the late New Testament concern for maintaining the purity of the faith. What more natural than a concern also to give the truth of that faith a solid basis? And what better basis for those familiar with Hebrew ways than that of providing witnesses? We have here, I think, an early manifestation of the same need that will be felt so acutely and brought to explicit thematization in the time of the Reformation and of Melchior Cano.

2. The Emerging Notion: Canon of Scripture, Ireneus, Tertullian, "Catholic" Tradition

The New Testament writings show a concern to specify the grounds and sources of the Christian word. Furthermore, they show the specification changing as time moves on. An early concern was to establish the meaning Jesus had for them and to corroborate their faith in him; in this context the appeal was to the Hebrew scriptures. Next, with faith in Jesus apologetically founded, the church of the missionary era a generation later rested its faith on the rock of the apostles who were bearers of the Christian word. Then the subapostolic church of the third generation refined this idea; the apostles came to be trusted as witnesses, appointed and reliable, of the events of the life, death, and resurrection of the Savior. All along the ultimate source remained the one true God and Jesus Christ whom he had sent. But there is a steady *redefining* of the *immediate* sources as the links with the ultimate and original sources come into clearer light. This will introduce a factor of some complexity into the subsequent history of the Christian word, and lead finally to the concept of the magisterium.

The chief phases of this further evolution are these. The early 2nd century begins to appeal to the apostolic writings as a distinct new source over and above the Hebrew scriptures and the apostolic witness. Implicit in such a procedure is the question of a new "canon" of scripture (though "canon" is anachronistic at this point). However, it takes time for that to become explicit: The apostolic writings have to achieve a footing of equality with the Old Testament, their inspiration has to be recognized, and the list of accepted books has to be at least roughly determined. But with the "canon" relatively fixed, a new need appears that we might call para-scriptural: Since heretics have recourse to the same scriptures as the orthodox church, and the task of refuting them is endless, the prior question has to be raised, To whom do the scriptures belong? Who has the right to use and interpret them? With this question we are well on the way to the concept of the magisterium and "Catholic" tradition.

Of course, the process did not unfold smoothly and systematically under the control of logic; it was rather a matter of a dialectical movement between persons who embodied the conflicting views. We are dealing with concrete history, and details and nuances are infinite; however, I am fortunate to be able to draw on the immense erudition of Campenhausen's work on the formation of the Christian canon.[11] There the reader will find three hundred densely packed pages dealing first with the vicissitudes of the Old Testament in Christian times, and then with the New Testament itself in four chapters entitled respectively:

The Pre-History of the New Testament Canon, the Emergence of the New Testament, Defining the Limits of the New Testament Canon, and The New Canon in Post-Irenaean Theology and in Origen.

The negative factors determining this history were mainly two unorthodox movements, the Marcionite and the Montanist. The pre-Marcionite church lacked "any formal authentication of the tradition which derives from and witnesses to Christ." The Christian simply presumed he knew Christ exactly as he was attested by the first disciples. What was taught in the congregation was accepted as authentic and original; when alien teachings occurred they were rejected on the ground of their disagreement with the tradition, but there was no method in the refutation. "Christians just 'know' the original truth; no one refers in support of it to texts and documents, regarded as an . . . established norm."[12] Along came Marcion, and the logic implicit in the use being made of the apostolic writings burst into life:

> Marcion's bible tabled once for all the question of a new canon, that is, the question of the "authentic" witnesses to the original gospel, which were to provide the standard of all later tradition and the norm for the preaching of the Church. The Church . . . could not ignore this question.[13]

It was Ireneus who did the needed work on the positive side to counteract Marcion. "He signalizes the transition from the earlier period of belief in tradition to the new age of deliberate canonical standardisation."[14] The novelty about his *Adversus haereses* is that quotations from the new scriptures are innumerable, replacing the proof formerly drawn from the Hebrew scriptures.[15] We saw in chapter three that he is "the first catholic theologian who dared adopt the Marcionite principle of a new 'scripture.' "[16] However, he "does not yet think in terms of a specific 'inspiration' of the New Testament writers."[17]

The second negative factor was Montanism which, simply by going too far under the impetus given by Ireneus, resulted in a salutary brake being applied. Ireneus was very influential; Clement of Alexandria, Tertullian, and Hippolytus all took up his idea of a new canon and developed it further. An immediate result, however, was a swift Montanist expansion in the number of books felt to be normative. Against Marcion, then, the church was expansive; but against Montanus the reaction was restrictive.[18] For the Montanists appealed, not to the new canon, but to the Spirit, who was newly poured forth and could not be less productive than the Spirit of past ages that produced the original scriptures.[19] New "scriptures" then began to proliferate, and

> the emergent catholic canon, which preserved the evidence of the beginnings, acquired all the greater importance . . . now it was seen as a sacred borderline beyond which no teaching or preaching ought ever to pass. . . .
> The "innumerable books" of the Montanist prophets, declares Hippolytus, only confuse the minds of those who are unable to test them, and for anyone of sound mind they are unworthy of attention.[20]

The reaction to Montanism reaches a plateau around A.D. 200 with the Muratorian fragment; it is the "first formal attempt at a definitive standardisation, and in principle marks the end of the long period of the formation of the Canon."[21]

This is as much of the vast researches of Campenhausen as it is to my purpose to quote. However, I must return to a question that he does not skimp but treats in the different perspective of his own purpose. Perhaps also he is somewhat concerned to see it in relation to the later controversy on scripture and tradition. It is the question that I called para-scriptural, for it deals with a problem not solved within scripture or by the fixing of the canon. It is a matter of the use of scripture; the question is: Who had the right to interpret it and what was one to do when heretics quote it to their own purpose? The question is raised explicitly, though in slightly different forms, by both Ireneus and Tertullian. Tertullian especially, Campenhausen concedes, saw the futility of endless exegesis to counteract heretical exegesis, and the need of a simpler and more effective procedure.[22] This is our question at the moment.

The *Adversus haereses* of Ireneus, for all its rambling diffuseness, reveals the new situation formed by ongoing history. The first chapter of the first book gives us the clue: Our adversaries, Ireneus says, "falsify the oracles of God, and prove themselves evil interpreters of the good word of revelation."[23] Remarks scattered through the first two books show this complaint to be continuously operative for Ireneus, but it is the third book, where he comes to his own positive statement, that concerns us most. His first chapter here states the source of all we know on "the plan of our salvation": the apostles, who first proclaimed the gospel and then committed it to writing. The next chapter lays the precise complaint against the adversaries: When we quote scripture, they appeal to tradition but, when we refer them to that tradition which originates with the apostles, they object to tradition. The third chapter reveals the strategy of Ireneus's reply: to list the order of succession from the apostles, through the bishops who followed them, down to the bishops of our own times, taking Rome as a sample. "In this order, and by this succession, the ecclesiastical tradition from the apostles, and the preaching of the truth, have come down to us."[24]

What Ireneus is doing, I should say, is moving from the objective to the subjective, not quite in the modern sense of "subjective" but in the sense that he turns from the truth itself to the bearer of that truth. He appeals directly neither to scripture nor to tradition though both of them contain the truth, but to the agents of the truth wherever it is found. Perhaps he has not got those categories quite clear or become fully aware of what is happening through his strategic decision, but it marks a significant trend in history, to be followed presently by Tertullian. Anyway, in his own mind he has found a principle to serve both for refutation and for proper procedure: "Since therefore we have such proofs, it is not necessary to seek the truth among others which it is easy to obtain from the church; since the apostles . . . lodged in her hands most copiously all things pertaining to the truth."[25]

Tertullian in his work *On Prescription against Heretics* brings the precision of legal argument to the point made more vaguely by Ireneus. The prior question is not what the scriptures say, but to whom the scriptures belong. To take the case to the court of the scriptures, with the adversaries quoting and interpreting them one way and the orthodox church another, is a useless procedure:

> To the Scriptures therefore we must not appeal . . . the order of things would require that this question should be first proposed, which is now the only one to be discussed, "To whom

belongeth the very Faith; whose are the Scriptures; by
whom, and through whom, and when, and to whom was that
rule delivered whereby men become Christians." For wherever both the true Christian rule and Faith shall be shewn to
be, there will be the true Scriptures, and the true expositions,
and all the true Christian traditions.[26]

Tertullian then, as the title of his work declares, is appealing to
prescription, a legal device in Roman law that had the effect of
not even allowing the case to come to court. As for positive
argument, he does not differ so very much from Ireneus. He
goes on, from the passage quoted, to speak of Christ commis-
sioning the apostles, the apostles founding churches, and other
churches deriving from the apostolic.[27] And he continues:

> On this principle therefore we shape our rule: that, if the
> Lord Jesus Christ sent the Apostles to preach, no others
> ought to be received as preachers than those whom Christ
> appointed. . . . Now what they did preach . . . must be
> proved in no other way than by those same Churches which
> the Apostles themselves founded.[28]

Concluding his work, Tertullian restates his general principle:
"And now indeed I have argued against all heresies in general,
that they ought to be forbidden by fixed, and just, and necessary
rules, to bring Scripture into their disputes."[29]

An enormous amount of learned ink has flowed in the effort
to analyze Ireneus and Tertullian. What matters here, however,
is the place of Ireneus and Tertullian in the ongoing evolution,
and that cannot be fully clarified by any interpretation of their
work, however erudite; it becomes plain only when the result of
the evolution has disclosed its direction. The direction of their
first fateful step turns out to be toward the doctrine of the magisterium; this doctrine will emerge in due course and reign with a
vengeance, only to be challenged in its own turn.

It is Athanasius, so much of whose work is concerned with
the explanation and defense of Nicea, who begins to bring the
next phase into focus. His *Letter on the Decrees of the Council
of Nicea*, the very title of which is itself significant, was written
about the year 350, and various phrases used by Athanasius
reveal the new state of the question: He talks about "the transac-

tions of the Council,"[30] and "the assembled Bishops,"[31] who "published against [the Arians] the sound and ecclesiastical faith."[32] Athanasius asks about them: "Are they not then committing a crime, in their very thought to gainsay so great and ecumenical a Council?"[33] The Arianizers are in the position of one condemned and arguing against the legitimate judge after the case is closed. (Athanasius too seems to have had his legal side.)

When we read Athanasius from the perspective of our question on the *loci*, and see his position as it appears in the trajectory we are plotting, his language is extremely significant. It is clear what the new state of the question is: The great council has become in some sense a "source" of the faith. Of course, we must insist again that it is not the ultimate source; Athanasius maintains as much as anyone could desire that the council did not invent the doctrine it promulgated.[34] The same point is made by contrast with the opponents of Nicea in his letter on the spurious synods of Ariminum in Italy and Seleucia in Isauria. This letter, *On the Synods*, written about 359, poked fun at their *dated* creed that gives the year of the consulate in which it was issued, and compared it with the great council of Nicea that simply wrote: "Thus believes the Catholic Church."[35] And repeatedly he accuses his adversaries of deserting "the Fathers."[36] But all his appeals to tradition cannot disguise the new state of affairs. Ireneus and Tertullian had appealed to the succession of bishops from the apostles onwards, but such a procedure is now impractical. The succession is too extended and the churches are too numerous. In any case, it would be useless when church is pitted against church. The one remedy now is an assembly of all the churches, where a consensus will prevail and the recalcitrant members be brought back into line. It is the *present* church beginning to assert itself as not only the legitimate heir of the past but also as a spokesman in its own right.

Let us designate what is emerging here by the term "Catholic tradition." I use it in contradistinction to apostolic tradition, hoping thereby to remove it from the controversy of the scripture/tradition dichotomy. It denotes simply the patrimony of dogmas defined by the church and made binding on her adherents, along with a train of lesser doctrines thought to be entailed by the dogmas. And the immediate source of these dogmas, always with an implicit or explicit appeal to the past for their ultimate justification, is the consensus of the present church, the "great church" as it came to be called in Athanasius's time. Nicea shows the mentality of this era as *vécu*; Augustine will make it *thématique* with his famous phrase "securus iudicat orbis terrarum."[37]

3. Full Thematization

A long interval separates Nicea from the Reformation. During most of it little thought was given to the question of *loci* which, in its own form, had so exercised Ireneus and Tertullian. Basil of Cesarea,[38] Augustine himself in another aspect of his thought,[39] Vincent of Lerins,[40] even Thomas Aquinas[41]—all of them could be included in a full and detailed history. But none of them, it seems to me, made the significant contribution to the forward movement of theology that we are looking for. This long repetitive period seems strange at first sight, but reflection may show it to be normal enough. On the one side there was the unparalleled development of the objective side of theology that the Middle Ages witnessed; with the wealth of patristic writings to draw on, and the seemingly inexhaustible fertility of the human mind to stimulate more and still more questions for the systematizing of that wealth, the theologians had enough to put all idle minds to work. On the other side, that of the agent of the word, there was no acutely felt need during all these centuries. Nicea had brought in the idea of the magisterium as the present agent for determining the faith; the church appeared as the authorized interpreter of God's word, legitimately linked with the past and recognized as the immediate source of dogma; why bother about more? In some societies, when needs are satisfied, inventions decline. There was little felt need for careful definition of the original sources, still less for determining their relation to the present, the theme that will occupy us in chapter five. The immediate source was enough; it told us all we know on earth about God's word, and all we need to know.

Nevertheless, there was a built-in source of tension on the subjective side of the situation, and perhaps history was waiting only for men's minds to tire of the mental gymnastics of systematic theology to bring it on the stage. The situation was this: The immediate voice and spokesman for God's word was in the present, but it had its authority only from the past and was legitimate only insofar as it maintained continuity with the past. Further, the all-important part of the past was the age of Christ and the apostles. It was rendered accessible through the scriptures but, as they receded further and further in time, the jump from scriptures into the present age became more and more a problem. The resulting tension appears in the late Middle Ages, and can be studied in the work of Oberman and others.[42] For my purpose it is sufficient to consult Paul De Vooght and his book on the sources of doctrine as they are revealed in the theologians of the 14th century.[43]

The period studied by De Vooght lies between 1317 and 1414, and marks the beginning of the trend toward treatises *de locis theologicis*. The background to the new stirring has a deceptive simplicity. In the Middle Ages the scriptures were the manual of theology (at least in principle—in practice the theologians wrote commentaries on Peter Lombard's *Sentences*). Further, casual statements made at the time would conclude logically to a doctrine of *sola scriptura*. Yet logic cannot really be applied at this point, before the terms are worked out and the premises accurately stated. Theologians may talk as if all their doctrine were in scripture but, when they come to difficult matters like the doctrine on the sacraments or that on the *Filioque*, they are capable of statements in the diametrically opposite direction: *multa non scripta*, or *non omne scriptum*. The situation has the confusion common in a time prior to thematization, when the question is not clearly stated.

It was William of Occam, according to De Vooght, who first put the clear question: Are all the truths necessary for salvation in the bible, or are they not? Occam gives reasons for both sides, but does not himself settle the question. Wycliffe goes farther and assumes his own fairly definite position. Finding himself in a situation where church and scripture seem to conflict, he is forced to think their relations through. His conclusion: Scripture and tradition come first, and then the church. He does not make a complete break with the past, but respects the normative function of traditional interpretation of scripture. His polemic, in fact, is more against pope and curia than against the church. Still the direction of his movement is clear and, since at the same time Henry of Totting is moving toward the other pole and extending the list of truths not found in scripture, the ways are dividing.[44]

Full polarization will come with the Reformation and the rebellion against the magisterium. Perhaps the Greek-Roman split a few centuries earlier should have precipitated the debate, and in a measure it did contribute: There was the Greek challenge to the "Apostles' " creed of the West,[45] there were the arguments over scriptural and patristic sources on the *Filioque,* and there was the role of the pope; all these were factors dividing the two sides. But the Greeks were farther away and spoke a different language; their withers were not wrung by the absurdities of late scholasticism. And so it was the Reformation that effectively polarized the positions, not so much in Luther's lifetime as later on in the opposition between Tridentine theologians and the Formula of Concord.

To find one's way through the literature on Luther nowadays is so arduous a task that a layman in the matter may be forgiven if he boldly states his case without deferring overmuch to the experts. I would say then that Luther stood for the principle that truth must be grounded, and that his lasting importance in this question lies there rather than in his particular attitude toward scripture. A more familiar way of putting it is to say that he reacted against mere arbitrary assertion and decree. Thus I find the following quotation significant; it is from a letter to Frederick, elector of Saxony, on Pope Leo's decretal, and was written about mid-January of 1519:

> Since in our day Holy Scriptures and the old teachers are reappearing and people everywhere in the world begin to ask not what but why this and that was said, were I to accept these mere words [of the decretal] and recant, my recantation would find no belief but would be looked upon as a mockery. . . . For what it [the decretal] says without any basis would not be established by my recantation.[46]

What impresses me in this passage is not the particular sources Luther refers to, scripture and the old teachers, but the idea itself of requiring an authority for one's statements, and the remark that this is the spirit of the times. On the further ques-

tion, Where is that authority to be found? Luther seems to have
been originally more flexible than his followers of half a century
later. The very letter I quoted expresses astonishment that Leo's
pronouncement was not based on a single sentence from
scripture or the fathers or canon law.[47] *Sola scriptura* seems, in
fact, to have become strict Lutheran doctrine only with the
Formula of Concord in 1577. One may consult Tappert's collection of early Lutheran confessions and find several references in
the index for the heading "Scriptures . . . the only judge, rule,
and norm of doctrine," but not one of these references is to the
Augsburg Confession, or the Apology of the Augsburg Confession, or to The Smalcald Articles, or to The Small Catechism, or
to The Large Catechism. The first reference is to the Formula of
Concord.[48]

Meanwhile the Catholic position was hardening in the opposite direction, though Trent itself, like Luther, retained a certain
flexibility. Its famous decree on the sources traces the gospel
through the prophetic promises, the preaching of the Lord Jesus
Christ, and the apostles, through whom finally it was to be
preached to everyone as the source of every salutary truth and
of every directive of conduct. Only in this context of the supre-
macy of the gospel as it was first preached do we meet the phrase
that has been found so provocative, that this truth and these
directives are contained in the written books and the unwritten
traditions that the apostles received from the Lord himself or
through the word of the Holy Spirit, and transmitted to us as if
from hand to hand. Even then, the phrase originally proposed for
the decree, *partly* in scriptures and *partly* in tradition, was rejected in favor of the more open formula we now have.[49] However, communications were not then what they are today.
Roman Catholic theologians needed a slogan to counter the
emerging *sola scriptura*, they thought to find it in the Tridentine
"scripture *and* tradition," and the two sides were soon at
loggerheads on the question. History now began to be written
with great diligence, but the diligence was exercised less on investigating the facts than on finding texts to prove the adversary
wrong. The painful centuries that followed are familiar to all.

It is here in these early decades of Lutheran-Catholic
polarization that I place the full focusing of the *loci* question, and

it happens that just then a work appears, called *De locis theologicis* and destined for long lasting influence. It is the composition of Melchior Cano, Dominican theologian and bishop, who died in 1560, leaving behind him for posthumous publication a work in twelve parts with the title quoted.[50] The idea of *loci* went back to Cicero, but Cano's immediate source was a Cologne work of 1527, *De inventione dialectica*, by Rudolph Agricola. The scope in Agricola was to find sources for arguments, but Cano rose above this debater's viewpoint: He was looking for grounds on which to base a judgment. Further, his range was liberating. He found seven sources for the judgments proper to theology, a discipline that is based on authority; they are scripture, the tradition of Christ and the apostles, the church (for Cano it is the "collectio omnium fidelium"), the councils, the popes, the fathers of the church, and finally the scholastic theologians and canonists. There are also three sources that constitute a "borrowed" set in theology: human reason, the philosophers and jurists, and finally history and human tradition.

The proliferation of "sources" in Cano suggest some concluding remarks for this chapter. We could say his range of sources harks back to what we saw of the real breadth of the New Testament. Now the New Testament was already hinting at a factor we shall have to study in chapter seven, the inner resources of judgment in the believer himself, collectively manifested in the *sensus fidelium* we are talking of more and more today. But Cano's range suggests another approach through analogy with Kant's categories. Kant found twelve a priori forms in the human mind with which he categorized all the materials delivered through the two channels of space and time. Then Lonergan came along to clear away the twelve categories and replace them with the single a priori of the heuristic nature of human spirit, the notion of being. Is there an analogy with the *sensus fidelium* that will replace all the categories of *loci*?

One thing at least I would hope, that the scripture/tradition controversy, which I have moved well out on the margins, will stay there permanently. Not that, with many today, I regard the question as meaningless; I think it has a meaning, but I do not regard it as the crucial area for inquiry and thought. That area I find much more broadly based. The whole effort to fix the *locus* or set of *loci* is a continually recurring manifestation of the pious longing to wrap the faith up in careful parcels. In the beginning there was just the good news along with the treasured words of the Lord. Soon the credentials of the apostles who bore the good news had to be established, and this was further specified by establishing their right to be witnesses, chosen in advance and appointed for the task. But as the living memory of the apostles became only a tradition the effort was to get a document from them or from their times that would possess their authority and be a kind of permanent presence in the church of those favored agents of the word. When the documents are found to present their own problem, there is a shift to the church as the owner of the documents, and the church in turn is successively epitomized in the fathers, in the great council, in the series of councils, and finally in the present church that here and now has authority to teach the word of God and interpret his meaning.

There was over and over again the effort to wrap up the faith in neat packages so that it could be delivered by registered mail. The basic oversight in it all was that the faith is a living thing and keeps growing. Just when you think you have it all wrapped up, something sticks out and you have to begin the process all over again. This was true in all the respecifications leading up to the church herself as the one immediate and sufficient source of doctrine. But it is true also of the reaction; when excessive attention to the subject preaching the word led to a rejection of the magisterium, the tearing off of all the later wrappings and going back to what seemed an original wrapping, the problem was not solved at all. You are still wrapping it up, and the wrapping is even more constrictive than before. This is roughly the situation with which we are left at the end of the *loci* era, and it leads directly to the next theme in the ongoing history of the word.

CHAPTER FIVE

THE SOURCES AS WORD
ACROSS SPACE AND TIME

Though my Introduction set forth six key transition-points in the history of the word, I do not see these six steps as of equal moment and significance; chapter four, for example, despite the way it looms up in books of controversy, shows a rather pedestrian advance in comparison with chapter three. With chapter five we come again to a transition of extreme importance, so much so that chapters six and seven, to which it introduces us, could be considered a unit set off against all the centuries represented by chapters three and four. The most revolutionary aspect of the new theology of the word could be put succinctly in terms drawn from Lonergan's intentionality analysis: It is a shift from the third level of consciousness to the fourth, from the cognitional to the affective (*Method*, passim). Of course, this represents a recovery of the original force of the word, so "revolutionary" must be taken here in its primary sense of coming back to the starting point. And yet we can never return to our origins in the frame of mind in which we left them; all the centuries devoted to the cognitional side of the word cannot simply be jettisoned. Furthermore, the questions that call forth the new stage arise out of the cognitional situation that developed in the way described in my two previous chapters, so we will look there for the clue that will launch us smoothly into the next stages of history.

That clue I find in a feature of the Christian message that tended to become submerged in the concentration on the message as word of God and his gift of truth, but began to move toward the surface again in the quest for *loci*. It is the particular local and temporal character of the message as originally delivered. As God's word it may be timeless and spaceless; at least we expect it, maybe are conditioned to expect it, to be as valid today in Toronto as it was nineteen centuries ago in Tarsus. And yet any word spoken by and through a human agent is bound to betray the particular conditions of the human speaker. We speak of these as the limitations of time and space, but in the original delivery of the word they represent not so much its limitations as its strength. A word of prophet or sacred writer is intended immediately for this defined circle of hearers or readers, and can be effective for them only if it is spoken in their language to their needs in their situation. So well is this understood today that it is taken for granted, until the contrary is proved, that writers speak to their contemporaries; only in such obviously exceptional and melodramatic cases as "Not to be opened till fifty years after my death" do we even pause to consider the contrary.

Now it is just under this heading that the uneasy balance of power in which the 16th-century controversies issued is seen to be precarious. Any community that exists across space and time but claims continuity with a beginning long ago and far away is sooner or later going to have to face the problem of reaching across that time and space to make an ancient and distant word effective in the here and now. This problem underlay the 16th-century feuds. The situation was in fact enormously different from that of the 1st century, and the word being preached differed correspondingly. When Luther made his challenge the Catholics might have replied, with the hindsight of today: There has been a development. But they knew little or nothing of developing cultural conditions and so instead took refuge in a vague appeal to tradition that did not stand up under examination. The Lutherans knew as little about changing times, and so fled back to the beginning, thinking to find in the written word that spanning of the centuries that all were seeking. But the permanence of the written word, its efficacity across space and time as this was once understood, has been exploded too, and both sides today face a new problematic.

I spoke just now of hindsight. If we exercise this marvelous power a little further we will see the problem operating incognito long before the 16th century; it is latent in the early days of the gospel after "the persecution that arose over Stephen." In the scattering that then took place the Christians spread the word, first "bringing the message to Jews only and to no others. But there were some natives of Cyprus and Cyrene among them, and these, when they arrived at Antioch, began to speak to pagans as well, telling them the good news of the Lord Jesus" (Acts 11:19-20). In this apparently innocuous statement the whole problematic of this chapter lies concealed. For the problem does not arise out of either space or time as such but out of the differences of culture. It is not just that *time* passes but that *times* change. New ways of life are begun, new needs arise, new questions are posed, new solutions sought, new ideas emerge. For the old words and the old ideas do not quite fit. Nathan thought out his parable for a particular situation, spoke his word to David, and thrust the message home with devastating simplicity: "You are the man" (2 Sam. 12:7). But the problem for all of us who read the scriptures today is to be able to say to ourselves as well as others: This is a word for you, precisely for you in precisely your situation.

It is a problem that has been gaining momentum for about a hundred years. It lies behind both the program of modernism in the late 19th century and the plea at the second Vatican council for *aggiornamento*. It is a factor too in the efforts of existential hermeneutics in the generation just past and equally a factor in the efforts to substitute a theology of the language-event for that form of hermeneutics. It is most articulate in the anguished cries of our students and laity for relevance in the word we speak to them. The problem, then, is recent, but that is to be expected; it could not really have surfaced before our century. First, time had to pass to separate us from the early days of the gospel. Second, times had to change to introduce new situations and the need of a new word. Third, and this is the real hurdle, there had to be a realization of this change, of the inadequacy of the old word in its old form, of the need of a new word adapted to our situation.

In fact, of course, the actual adaptation kept taking place all along, though without explicit awareness of what was occurring. It was taking place all along, not only when the natives of Cyprus and Cyrene began to speak to the pagans as well as to the Jews, but long before that in the ancient history of the Jewish word, and long afterwards right up to last Sunday's sermon, when the preacher said: Let us apply that word to our own situation. It is that actual adaptation that will supply us with the materials with which we begin each chapter, the elements as they exist *vécu* in the sources; we will also look, as usual, for the incipient thematizing that gradually brings the new phase of history into full focus.

1. The New Testament Quest for Understanding

The theme of this chapter is the efficacity of the word across space and time. But, for those who would respond to a word in a human way, a condition of its efficacity is that it be understood, and in fact it is lack of this understanding that we experience most keenly when we are distant from the source. No doubt there are other conditions of efficacity, on the side of both speaker and hearer; but one thing at a time, and we are starting within the cognitional context that history has provided. From that viewpoint we have to say, then, that the real problem is not spatio-temporal; it is one of understanding, and that is the category we will try to find in the New Testament. I believe that we do find this theme anticipated in the scriptures, both in the quest for understanding revealed there and, to some extent, in the descriptions of its attainment.

The quest for understanding is expressed, quite fittingly, in questions. I delay for a moment to remark how extraordinary it is that we have paid so little attention to the question as an activity of the believing mind in the scriptures. There are dictionary articles on the term "to question" as it occurs in the New Testament, but they are short compared to the articles on "confess," "witness," and the like. And there is practically nothing on the activity of questioning that occurs so frequently in the living reality and is recorded in the pages of the scriptures with far ampler illustration than the activity of confessing or witnessing.

We begin with Paul. The seventh chapter of 1 Corinthians opens with the phrase: "And now for the matters you wrote about." It turns out that these matters were practical questions put to him, questions in this chapter on marriage, celibacy, virginity, and questions on other matters following in later chapters. Further, the questions do not admit of an answer merely by quoting a word from the Lord; sometimes, most frequently, I would say, there is no word from the Lord and Paul has to think

out the answer. It is instructive to follow Paul's progress as he
takes up a question: "After all, what is Apollos? What is Paul?"
(1 Cor. 3:5); and a long answer is developed through an entire
chapter and more, with Paul concluding: "Into this general picture, my friends, I have brought Apollos and myself on your
account, so that you may take our case as an example" (1 Cor.
4:6). To follow Paul through this exercise of understanding is to
realize that we are assisting at a thinking out of the role of the
apostle in relation to God and to Christ. The answer was not in
what was handed down, not explicitly anyway. Paul had to work
it out. The impetus to work it out is supplied by the question, and
the achievement itself results in a new understanding.

With Mark we are in a different situation. Questions found
in Paul had to do with church life, with Paul's own ministry, with
God's purposes in regard to Israel, etc. But in Mark the questions converge around the one great question of who and what
Jesus is: "Who can this be whom even the wind and the sea
obey?" (4:41). The questions begin with one put by the unclean
spirit on his role and purpose: "What do you want with us, Jesus
of Nazareth?" (1:24). The first question put by the people concerns the teaching of Jesus: "What is this? A new kind of teaching!" (1:27). The series continues with questions about his wisdom and power and authority (6:2; 6:3; 11:28). It comes to a kind
of climax with the question of the High Priest, "Are you the
Messiah, the Son of the Blessed?" (14:61), and that of Pilate, "Are
you the king of the Jews?" (15:2). Emphatically Jesus appears in
the gospel of Mark as one who was a question—to the Jews, to
Pilate, to the spirits, and to the young Christian church.

If Mark illustrates the extraordinary proliferation of questions about Jesus, Luke can serve to illustrate the process of
reaching an answer. A kind of pattern is supplied in the story of
the disciples on their way to Emmaus at Easter. Jesus joined
them, found them quite without understanding of recent events
or of the prophecies, and so he "explained to them the passages
which referred to himself in every part of the scriptures" (Lk.
24:27). In the sequel to the story he goes through the same explanation to the Eleven and the others. "Then he opened their
minds to understand the scriptures" (24:45). The Acts of the
Apostles give a second instance: It is in the way the Christians

came to understand the calling of the nations to share in the gospel. It must have been a giant step in their eyes, if we may judge from the attention Luke gives it. He prepares the ground by a careful history of the way the church actually came to preach to the Gentiles (Acts 8:4ff.; 8:26ff.; ch. 10; etc.), puts the question forward as one hotly debated (ch. 11), adduces a vision given to Peter to justify the step, and continues with the precedent-setting remark we have seen: "But there were some natives of Cyprus and Cyrene . . . and these . . . began to speak to pagans as well" (11:20).

Luke's accounts inform us in a telescoped way how the church came to understand, by a slow process extending presumably over a period of years, two very central concerns, who Jesus is and what the church's mission is. We have now to ask to what extent the New Testament writers moved toward a thematization of that process. One thing is clear: They were explicitly aware of human inquiry into the meaning of God's deeds and words. Two passages bring this out beautifully. One that we saw already is worth seeing again from our new perspective: "This salvation was the theme which the prophets pondered and explored. . . . They tried to find out what was the time, and what the circumstances, to which the spirit of Christ in them pointed . . . and it was disclosed to them that the matter they treated of was not for their time but for yours" (1 Pet. 1:10-12). Three verbs denoting inquiry tumble over one another in a little cascade as Peter tries to put the point across: pondered, explored, tried to find out. My second, much shorter but no less significant, quotation: "But Mary treasured up all these things and pondered over them" (Lk. 2:19). The Greek word for "ponder" in this text is the same one used to describe the Sanhedrin debate in Acts 4:15; that is, there was a discursive process back and forth in Mary's mind as she tried to understand.

May I hope that this kind of background would help advance those word-studies that pertain to the incipient thematizing of our question but must be omitted here and left to the specialists. I am thinking of "see" in the religious sense of Isaiah: "You will look and look and never see" (Mt. 13:14), and in the deeper layers of meaning noticed when John makes seeing Jesus equivalent to knowing him as Son (14:7-10).[1] I am thinking of "know" in its complex Hebrew meaning, and in the differentiated sense of "the man who knows the good he ought to do and does not do it is a sinner" (Jas. 4:17), and again in the deep Johannine sense: "We speak of what we know" (3:11); "If you knew me you would know my Father" (14:7). But mostly I am thinking of the Greek verbs with their various compounds and cognates, which are translated in English by "understand": "When a man hears the word . . . but fails to understand it . . ." (Mt. 13:19). "Then they understood: they were to be on their guard" (Mt. 16:12). "But they understood nothing of all this; they did not grasp what he was talking about; its meaning was concealed from them" (Lk. 18:34). "Then he opened their minds to understand the scriptures" (Lk. 24:45).

I am sure that, when scholars say "the problem of understanding is not intellectual, but existential," one of "hardness of heart,"[2] they have a point and know what they are talking about, but I would ask if it is necessary to exclude completely the intellectual element, even in the Marcan passage in question here. As for the other passages I quoted, it is surely not just my Catholic piety toward Mary that convinces me it was not her hardness of heart that made her slow to understand, and I would say the same about the Old Testament prophets who pondered and explored so laboriously before they came to understand the message. Surely there is question of an object that is hidden, mysterious, hard to fathom, question too of a mental activity of wondering, debating, supposing, and reflecting, and question finally of a breakthrough to an insight that combines intelligence and understanding with religious experience.

2. Reinterpreting the Word of God

One particular aspect of this quest for understanding deserves special study. It pertains especially to the understanding of the word of God in the scriptures but refers to the word of Jesus too, and could be described as an effort to reinterpret the message and apply it to new situations. It is operative in the very writing of the scriptures where it takes the form of *rewriting* the previous message. Once the canon of the scriptures was fixed and the *sacra pagina* had become a holy thing not to be tampered with, that rewriting naturally was unthinkable; but the same thrust appeared in the unleashing of a hermeneutic that found inexhaustible depths of meaning in the ancient word. One way or another the underlying purpose remained the same: reinterpretation for our times and application to our situation. Not that this was necessarily made explicit in the minds of the exegetes of the word; it was again the *vécu* that we have found over and over to be so significant for the history of theology.

Pierre Grelot describes the attitude and procedures of the Hebrew exegetes, especially after the dispersal, when their people had but their faith and law and cult to unite them and searched the scriptures where that faith and law and cult were recorded. The objective was to discover what the scriptures said to them in their own times and circumstances; it was to make the scriptures relevant; in the French expression, it was to *actualiser* the scriptures, to give them *valeur de vie*. To this end a chain of writings appeared in the form of what is called *midrash* (from the verb, *darash*, which connotes a search) and divides into three types: *halakka*, which sought in the Torah above all a juridical rule of conduct, and so belonged especially to the learned as well as to the pietists; *haggada*, which sought especially a spiritual formation and found place most of all in the synagogue; and *pesher*, which sought to make the prophecies of scripture contemporary, to show their fulfillment in events of the recent past or present. In this work the exegete compared text with text, tried analysis of words, had recourse to living tradition; but above all he was guided by his global sense of the meaning of revelation. In the Alexandrian milieu he also tried Greek tools of exegesis, especially the allegory that was to have such a fateful history in Christian times.[3]

New Testament use of the Old would certainly be an instance of such rereading, and an important one for our history. Our chapter on *loci* already adverted to the Christian practice, but it is relevant to add two points now. The first is that the Christians sometimes took liberties with the sense of the Old Testament to discover in it a reference to Christ or a prophecy of some particular episode in his life.[4] The second is that they introduced already the use of allegory—not to any extent, but the precedent was given and the principle established.[5]

Within New Testament times the practice continues in at

least three ways. One is parallel to the Old Testament rewriting of the text; we do not expect to find much of this in a set of documents produced within the short span of two or three generations, but the use Matthew and Luke make of Mark would be one important instance.[6] A second goes back to Mark and spans oral and written forms of the message; it is the editing of the tradition that is studied in redaction-criticism.[7] The third goes back beyond Mark himself to the practices that are studied in form-criticism, and here the purpose of adaptation is particularly in evidence. The name "form-criticism" is derived from the objective, "to trace the *provenance* and assess the historicity of particular passages by a close analysis of their structural forms."[8] But it is the assumption behind this work that interests me: "The vital factors which gave rise to and preserved these forms are to be found in the practical interests of the Christian community."[9] That is, the community *adapted* the message to their situation and needs. For example, when Jesus said, "Behold my mother and my brothers," he had the immediate circle of listeners in mind; they were his mother and brothers. "But as the narrative stood it was of no practical use as an appeal in preaching. It was necessary to add a universal application which would bring in would-be converts. Hence a preacher added the words 'Whosoever shall do the will of God, the same is my brother, and sister, and mother.' "[10]

One could delay here, and discuss to what extent the ideas implicit in these practices became explicit in the minds of the early believers and bearers of the message. It could be a very profitable discussion, provided we remained aware of the slight distortion thereby introduced into the picture. To speak, as I did a moment ago, of the effort to make the scriptures relevant is to veer from the target. The scriptures for our ancestors are automatically relevant, simply because they are from God and contain an inexhaustible wealth of meaning.

That was certainly the view that prevailed in the exegesis of post-scriptural times, which I propose to cover now in a rapid survey.[11] A factor already of prime significance in the Hebrew dispersal was the invasion of allegory due to intermingling with the surrounding Greek populations: "Those who lived outside Palestine had a tendency to make the Bible say what their more enlightened neighbors said."[12] To this end they borrowed the allegorical method the Greek philosophers had introduced to give an acceptable meaning to the myths of their tradition. The method was all the more acceptable because of the militant anti-Jewish attitude of men like Marcion. These attacked the Old Testament with vigor, and Christians responded with an allegorical interpretation of the offensive passages.

But a counter-movement developed, maybe as a reaction to excessive allegorizing after the Marcionite danger had passed, and a sharp division developed between the schools of Alexandria and Antioch. Alexandria had been the city of Philo, and his influence is probably to be seen in Clement and Origen; at any rate this school set out to overcome the anthropomorphic passages of the Old Testament: They would spiritualize the scriptures.[13] The school of Antioch, already literal in tendency and made more so by study of the biblical languages, reacted against this excess. Thus, the representative Theodore of Mopsuestia, insisting on literalism, declared that most of the Old Testament prophecies referred to future events within Jewish history rather than to Christ. Actually, Theodore's results were not so different from those of Alexandria: "One reason for this similarity is to be found in the fact that typology, which he frequently employs, is not entirely unlike allegorization. Again, he constantly stresses the metaphorical meaning of passages of scripture, while continuing to regard this meaning as literal."[14] Both schools found a channel to the Western theology of the Middle Ages, one through Jerome who derived much of his method from Antioch, the other through Augustine, who needed allegory to be at home in traditional Christianity.[15]

The Middle Ages, however, had their own preoccupations, and applied their bent for system to the meaning of scripture too. From Origen, through John Cassian, they derived the view of a fourfold meaning. Two meanings are basic, the historical or literal, and the spiritual; but the spiritual has three subspecies: tropological or moral, allegorical, and anagogical. An old Latin couplet explains the four: "The letter tells what happened, allegory what you are to believe, the moral sense tells you what you are to do, and the anagogical where you are heading."[16] Sober theologians used the three spiritual senses with circumspection.

Thomas Aquinas, for example, expressly made the literal meaning basic and insisted that it alone can furnish an argument. Nicholas of Lyra, author of the first bible commentary ever printed, became a force for literal interpretation through his influence on Luther, as the latter confesses: "When I was a monk, I was an expert in allegories. I allegorized everything. . . . So I hated Lyra . . . because he so diligently pursued the literal meaning. But now . . . I place him ahead of almost all interpreters."[17]

And yet, the divine dissatisfaction with a merely literal meaning remained. Blackman gives expression to it in his work on biblical interpretation.[18] Barth and others talked of a "pneumatic" exegesis of the scriptures,[19] and Roman Catholic exegetes and theologians went through a period of favor for the *sensus plenior*.[20] This plenary meaning was one that the human author did not conceive but the divine author did; it was therefore a real meaning of scripture, for it was the one intended by the principal author. But, while it was never used as immoderately as allegory, it was just as little subject to control, for it was not specified by any empirical basis in the text.[21] Finally, we may mention the *sensus consequens*,[22] the meaning the church developed by way of conclusions from the scripture. This is easier to control, but it is not a real meaning of scripture in the way scientific exegesis has to understand the term. However, it can serve here as transitional to Newman's notion of development, with which it has a certain kinship.

3. New Things and Old: The Development of Doctrine

The long history we have surveyed of rereading, rewriting, and reinterpreting the word of God testifies to the enduring sense of the believer that God is not the God of the past but of the present. He still speaks, he has not left us without help in our time of need. But it testifies too, in a less explicit way, to the increasing difficulty the believer felt in relating that word to his present time and present need. When reinterpreting replaced the now unthinkable rewriting, he had one way or another to postulate a surplus of meaning over and above the literal sense, which was seen with growing clarity to be related directly to a particular people at a particular time in a particular situation. Only the most reactionary fundamentalist would deny that element of particularity today, so sensitive have we grown to the variations of history and to the cultural differences that appear as we cross borders in space and time. But efforts to define this surplus meaning seemed to have failed; allegorization had come into contempt, and both the pneumatic exegesis of the Protestants and the plenary sense of the Catholics were dying a natural death. Was there any further avenue to explore?

To many Catholics of our generation, certainly to me in the early years of my work in theology, it seemed that Newman with his notion of the development of doctrine was the man of the hour with an idea that might complement the struggles of literal exegesis. Not that Newman had such a program in mind—he himself conceived his work to meet a difficulty,[23] not to initiate a program; not even that his idea was immediately relevant to the problem and to a full solution, but that it contained virtualities that could be exploited. As we have said, contemporaries do not, and generally cannot, know what is happening in and through them. Newman had himself talked of the virtualities of a great idea and built his own notion upon that basis; why not, therefore, apply to him what he had conceived in regard to others? Why not a development, not only in patristic times, but in the very present? a development that would be the equivalent, at least as far as the content of the word went, to the voice of the prophet among us again?

We should not underestimate the difficulty such a program would have in winning the grudging assent of conservative believers. No one I know of, in all the long history of exegesis, had dreamed of saying the word of God might change. After all, the Hebrew symbol for truth was rock, and the scriptures were full of that symbolism. God himself was he with whom "there is no variation, no play of passing shadows" (Jas. 1:17). Quite naturally his word shared this character. "It is impossible that the word of God should have proved false" (Rom. 9:6). Not only that, it remains even if heaven and earth should pass away (Mk. 13:31). "But the word of the Lord endures forevermore" (1 Pet. 1:25). Scripture, of course, was the example *par excellence* of such permanence: "Scripture cannot be set aside" (Jn. 10:35).

And so the prevailing attitude of the believer, from the 1st century to the 20th, was that of the Pastorals; "Timothy, keep safe that which has been entrusted to you" (1 Tim. 6:20). "Guard the treasure put into our charge" (2 Tim. 1:14).

Newman was as devoted as anyone to the word of God and to the treasure that had been entrusted to the church. He was not in any sense preaching a new revelation to replace an obsolescent old one, but he was affirming a new thing under the heavens and, when we remember that he had left one church and was not fully accepted yet by the other, we can understand a little better the slow progress his notion of development made in theological circles.

Actually there was a fairly clear, if remote and somewhat tainted, precedent for Newman's idea: It went back to Origen. We may recall here the passage quoted in chapter three, where Origen speaks of doctrines on which the apostles kept silence, "their intention undoubtedly being to supply the more diligent . . . with an exercise on which to display the fruit of their ability." He goes on to list the doctrines we believe, and to add a catalogue of disputed questions, "matters which we must investigate to the best of our power from holy scripture, inquiring with wisdom and diligence."[24] But this mentality found little echo in the fathers of the church. Athanasius, defending the Nicene *homoousios*, did not appeal to development but maintained that the church was compelled by the Arianizers to adopt the term "consubstantial" in order "to concentrate the sense of the Scriptures."[25] Augustine is of the same mind; when doctrines are attacked they "are studied more diligently and understood more clearly and preached more insistently, and so, from the fact that adversaries raise a question, we derive an occasion for learning."[26] As for Vincent of Lerins, a reactionary if ever there was one, his famous phrase on development is simply a concession grudgingly made: "It must be that understanding, knowledge, and wisdom grow. . . . But with the same kind of dogma, frame of mind, and intellectual approach."[27] One has only to read the *Commonitories* to see how much the "but" is characteristic of Vincent, and how little the "must . . . grow" represents his mind.

In modern times, according to Chadwick, there have been

two efforts to deal with the data that Newman will later analyze more successfully. Bossuet held that variation in the teaching of the faith must be a sign of error. Progress of doctrine in this case means, not deeper understanding, but evangelistic success. As for the definitions of faith promulgated by the church, they are simply a matter of clarification and explication; that is, they translate into clear language what the church already knows in other terms. The second theory is that of logical explanation: Definition of a doctrine is explicating what was implicit, and in this way also medieval scholastics could defend the unity of faith in Old Testament and New; the former implicitly contained the latter. But when theologians after Trent began to analyze this "logical explanation," they ran into such difficulties that the theory broke down. For one thing, they had to explain how a "natural" premise could join forces with a premise from revelation to yield a conclusion that must be believed with divine faith. For another, such "logic" made historical inquiry superfluous. Various eccentric theories now began to emerge, but it was only with Newman that a third force came into play besides Bossuet and the scholastics.[28]

The specific influence on Newman derived from the culture and thinking of the 19th rather than the 17th century. Darwin's *The Origin of Species* came out only in 1859, but his voyages on the Beagle took place between 1831 and 1836, he was publishing long before his book appeared, and the cast of mind to which it gave expression in the field of biology was already forming more widely. In the historical field too, maybe even more than in the biological, the idea of development was in the air. In the Catholic faculty of theology at Tübingen it found expression in the idea of tradition as a living force instead of a set of doctrines handed on secretly. Möhler's *Die Einheit der Kirche* . . . was published in 1825, and Möhler himself had been preceded by Drey. There does not seem to have been direct dependence of Newman on Tübingen, but one may say that their very independence of one another is a witness to the way the idea had permeated the culture and thinking of the time.[29]

Newman broached his idea in a sermon on the feast of the Purification in 1843,[30] and the work that everyone knows, *An Essay on the Development of Christian Doctrine*, came out two years later. The book is a kind of apologetic for the Catholic church, at least in the sense of a self-understanding by which one takes account of one's faith. Newman is dealing with the problem of continuity and change not in a programmatic way, but to meet a difficulty. He did not doubt the fact of continuity in change, but he had to explain it to himself in order to be at peace with his conscience. There were, he saw, "apparent variations," "apparent inconsistencies and alterations" in the doctrine and worship of the church.[31] He accepted these variations as simple historical fact, not therefore to be challenged as fact. But he labored to explain the fact, and his concentration was on the virtualities of any great idea that was contained in revelation and was susceptible of development:

> When an idea . . . is of a nature to arrest and possess the mind, it may be said to . . . live in the mind which is its recipient.
>
> [The] process . . . by which the aspects of an idea are brought into consistency and form, I call its development, being the germination and maturation of some truth or apparent truth on a large mental field.[32]

The condition of possibility of such development is the virtuality contained in the idea: "Its beginnings are no measure of its capabilities, nor of its scope. At first no one knows what it is, or what it is worth."[33]

But the proof of such a mental pudding is in its elaboration and application to the concrete, and Newman must tackle that. Weigel outlines his tactics for us:

> In the light of an unsystematic social psychology he sets up certain patterns for change within an identical flow. First, identity in change preserves its substantial form throughout all the changes. Second, the same principles of life and thought are continuously dynamic. Third, the identical thing in change organically assimilates into itself new elements. Fourth, it draws forth from its own principles new conclusions rendered imperative by its own growth. Fifth, the earlier stage already shows anticipations of later developments. Sixth, newer patterns of being are the result of clinging faithfully to original principles thrust into new contexts. Seventh, at any moment the identical continuum is present with the vigor of life.[34]

Then, through seven chapters, Newman applies the elements of this pattern to the life and doctrine of the early church.[35]

By and large the work of Newman, viewed with suspicion at home and with indifference abroad, fell to the ground with a dull thud. Those who did take up his idea at the turn of the century did not help his cause very much, for they themselves were branded modernist. But two extremist movements on the continent may be said to have clarified the development question by overstepping the boundaries. In 1919 Tuyaerts published a book that carried the logical idea to its logical extreme. Theological conclusions seemed to be for him the sort of thing one could derive from feeding premises into a logic-machine; on the material side, almost every article of the *Summa theologiae* of Saint Thomas could become a dogma.[36] There was an inevitable reaction to the opposite extreme. In 1938 L. Charlier published a book in which he showed himself to be a deadly enemy of theological conclusions. Given that Christ is a man, we cannot conclude at all that he has a human will, etc. There is development, and a law of development, but we do not know this law, nor can we discover the present faith implicit in the past. All we can do is trust the magisterium of the church. The magisterium responded to this theory by putting Charlier's volume on its index of prohibited books.[37]

In the end, however, Newman came into his own as a theologian. France, the Lowlands, and Germany began to take an interest in his ideas and, when three International Newman Conferences had been held, his followers in England felt it was time "to bring Newman home"; the result in 1966 was the first Oxford Newman Symposium.[38] He is assured, then, of his own place in the history of doctrine that he loved and knew so well. That does not mean that his ideas are accepted uncritically. After a period of suspicion and a wave of enthusiasm, it is possible to take a more moderate view: The fact of development that he brought to our attention is acknowledged, and it explains a good deal of doctrinal history. But it by no means explains it all. Chapters six and seven will show other forces that must be brought to bear on the complex history of the Christian word.[39]

4. Adaptation of the Word to the Present: Modernism

Newman, as far as I know, did not in his thinking on development have adaptation to present needs as his purpose. He was meeting a difficulty; the difficulty arose out of an apparent divergence, somewhere in the past, from the true and genuine Christianity of the apostles; to meet it one had to enter into the past and see what had really happened. But the idea of authentic development, once it had been formulated, became available for that further purpose of adaptation. If there was development in the past, presumably it occurred in response to a need of the times; if it met a need arising in the past, why should it not meet similar needs arising in the present? In other words the virtualities of Newman's idea extend to the field of *aggiornamento*, as it was called in Pope John's time, or modernism as it was called at the turn of the century. It was the modernists, especially the Roman Catholic branch of the movement, who appealed to Newman for their justification, and added to Newman's work the element needed to bring the next stage of our history after *loci* to full thematization.[40]

It would be remarkable that this idea took so long to emerge, had we not become accustomed to the slow progress of the believing mind. I mentioned earlier the ever-efficient hindsight with which we can see now that it was very much part of the *vécu* in early Christian times, from that fateful day when the natives of Cyprus and Cyrene began to speak to the pagans as well as to the Jews about the Lord Jesus (Acts 11:20-21). For, however little this may have been recognized, it involved recasting the message. Thus, the Palestinian "Son of Man" drops entirely from Paul's terminology (how could one explain this very Hebrew term to the Greeks?) to be replaced by the more intelligible term, Son of God. And the adaptation that form-criticism postulates in the transmission of particular gospel passages is there almost patently in the description Luke gives of Paul's missionary sermons. When he is talking to the Jews at Pisidian Antioch, Paul begins with Israelite history: "The God of this people of Israel chose our fathers" (Acts 13:17). A little later at Lystra he is evangelizing pagans and says nothing of Israelite history or the God of Israel; rather he speaks of the God who made heaven and earth, who "has not left you without some clue to his nature . . . he sends you rain from heaven and crops in their seasons" (14:17). And later still, preaching to the sophisticated pagans of Athens, he speaks much more deeply of the divine nature and of man's relationship to God, even quoting their pagan poets: "In him we live and move, in him we exist; as some of your own poets have said, 'We are also his offspring' " (17:28).[41]

What Paul did as the Christian message moved out of its Palestinian matrix into the very different world of the Greek-speaking peoples, the modernists tried to do in order to bring the Christian message across the boundaries from the medieval world into the modern:

> "Modernism" in Christian thought designates those theologies which are concerned with reinterpreting traditional Christian beliefs so as to make them intelligible in the light of the scientific understanding of the world and of historical knowledge. Modernism thus seeks to establish the relevance of Christian doctrine to the experience of modern man.[42]

The key word here is *relevance*; it defines the purpose of modernism. And the two phrases that fix the problem are *scientific understanding* and *historical knowledge*; they indicate the difference between our world and the medieval, a difference surely comparable to that between Palestinian and Greek in ancient times.

The movement shares with liberalism the desire and effort to be modern but was more concerned, at least in the early Roman Catholic phase, to take account of tradition as well. Thus Loisy's *L'Evangile et l'Eglise*, a work that seemed to the conservatives to have opened Pandora's box of heresies, was actually written against the liberal Protestant Harnack and his substitution of an "essence" of Christianity for the living tradition:

> Harnack, by identifying Christianity with a single, timeless idea, had failed to realize that a religion is a living, growing, dynamic movement which gradually unfolds its meaning, and does not necessarily disclose its essence at its origin.[43]

A further point of opposition to liberal Protestantism was formulated by Tyrrell as that movement's "bland faith and hope in the present order, its refusal to face the incurable tragedy of human life."[44]

But the precise interest of my study lies in the modernist idea of adaptation to the present. Let me return to Loisy, again as quoted by Vidler:

> There is no institution on earth nor in human history, whose legitimacy and value could not be contested, if it be laid down as a principle that nothing has a right to exist except what was in its original condition. This principle is contrary to the law of life, which is a movement and a continual effort of adaptation to perpetually changing and new conditions. Christianity could not escape this law, and it is not to be blamed for having submitted to it. It could not do otherwise.[45]

One further quotation from Vidler to clinch the point:

> That the Catholic Church has adapted the gospel and is adapting it still, that it adapts itself continually to the needs of new times, is by no means evidence that it forgets the gospel or slights its own tradition, but that it wants to make both prevail, that it realizes they are flexible and always perfectible.[46]

It does not belong to my understanding of history to evaluate the modernists in their personal responsibility for the sad and tragic end to which they and their movement came, or to evaluate the hierarchy that condemned them and their work, or even to evaluate the doctrinal positions assumed by one side or the other. But it *is* part of my task to say that they mark a transition to a distinct new phase of the theology of the Christian word. They brought into focus, and would have introduced into explicit consciousness in Catholic studies, an element that was implicit in the exegetical practices of long centuries, that was overlooked in the desperate search of the *loci* period for contact with the sources, and that might have animated a new period of communication of the word very much in the spirit of the second Vatican council. That is not by any means to give them the final judgment in theology; other factors keep emerging in the restless advance of history. We shall turn to them in chapters six and seven, after looking at a Protestant counterpart of the Catholic modernist effort.

5. "Today if you hear his voice":
The Protestant Way

An element of the word has been missing from explicit consciousness since the end of chapter two: the character of address, call, demand for a response, the personal factor. It disappeared, or at least receded into the background, when truth became the theme; it remained lost to view in the *loci* phase; and it was not restored by the Catholic efforts of the 19th century to bring the word into our century. Newman's work on development was not at all directed to meeting such a need,[47] and though the modernists were definitely moving in the right direction with their plea for relevance, they did not sufficiently thematize that aspect of call or address which was a feature of the biblical word: "Today if you hear his voice, do not grow stubborn" (Heb. 4:8).

This missing element is supplied in the Protestant counterpart to the Catholic work on development, most prominently in two German trends of our own day, the existential interpretation of Bultmann, and the "new hermeneutic" of some of the post-Bultmannians.[48] Fundamentally, I should think, the impulse and interest would derive from Luther's reverence for the preached word, and his scorn of scholastic system in favor of a Christ who is Christ "for me."[49] It would have a kinship with Kierkegaard's flat assertion, against all scientific efforts to make contact with Christ, that we *are* his contemporaries through faith.[50] And Kierkegaard gave it as his view that the best sermon we could preach would be to rise in the pulpit, read a passage of scripture, stand there in silence for a few minutes, and then step down.[51] But this robust way of sweeping the problem aside could hardly satisfy the modern need for giving an account of the word we hear, and so a renewed effort was mounted in the 20th century. If the Catholic effort was especially at home with the mentality that took revelation as a message, the Protestant is closer to the notion of revelation as a deed, but that is not precisely the theme at the present time.

Bultmann's view, expressed after his statement of the difficulties for modern man in the mythological framework of the New Testament message, is

> that the real purpose of New Testament myth is not to give an objective picture of the world but to express man's self-

understanding. Myth is not to be interpreted as a picture of
the cosmos but as a means by which the writers understand
themselves. As a result, we must not ask whether the myth
correctly describes the universe but whether it is a true understanding of human existence.[52]

Bultmann's answer is that the bible does give such an understanding, and tells me things about my own existence that vitally
concern me; more than that, it calls me to respond:

> The Bible not only shows me, like other historical docu-
> ments, a possible way of understanding my own existence, a
> way which I am free to accept or reject: more than that, it
> assumes the shape of a word which addresses me person-
> ally.[53]

There are, it seems, two elements in this address. On one side
there is my own preunderstanding *(Vorverständnis),* which gives
me a common ground of understanding with the sacred writer; if
we are to understand Socrates' death, we must first know what it
means to die.[54] But that is not enough to constitute actual address; that side "is something which I cannot anticipate or take
into account as a systematic principle for my exposition. For, in
traditional language, that is the work of the Holy Ghost."[55]

These two elements are surely among the conditions of possibility for hearing the ancient word of God as a word addressed
to me today; I will return to them in due course. But they still
leave a great gap to be filled in regard to the message itself. Many
of us are unhappy with Bultmann's analysis of the New Testament message simply in terms of the self-understanding it gives
me. His position has come under fire as dispensing with history
and content. For Bultmann, the case is as follows:

> In the proclamation of the gospel we do not meet Jesus as a
> person of past history; we meet him as the "eschatological
> phenomenon" who forces us to a decision. All that we need
> to know about Jesus is that he came and died and is now
> proclaimed by the church as Lord and Savior. To ask for
> more historical knowledge of Jesus is to seek salvation by
> works.[56]

Is there, then, any way of going beyond Bultmann in this
renewed Protestant effort to make the word a word for us today?

The proponents of the "new hermeneutic" have thought that there is. In Bultmann's view, my own self-understanding is involved as preunderstanding in the task of interpretation, but it is still we who are active and the text that is passive; our self-involvement is subordinate to the purpose of interpreting the text. Not so in the new hermeneutic; now the text interprets us. In older interpretation we interrogate the text, but in the new the text interrogates us.[57] It seems that the active and passive roles are reversed. Again, Bultmann's hermeneutic was away from language back to the understanding that was prior to and more authentic than language;[58] the new hermeneutic would supplement his work with a more positive correlation between language and interpretation.

The philosophy behind these renewed efforts, as they appear in Gerhard Ebeling and Ernst Fuchs, is that of the "later" Heidegger. Bultmann had followed the "early" Heidegger, and the analysis of human existence given in the latter's *Sein und Zeit*; but the later Heidegger has either taken a new direction or else developed very extensively the latent direction of his earlier work. The human element so prominent in *Sein und Zeit* now seems to disappear before some mysterious figure named "Being." Further, language is linked with this Being, and the link is described in a way that is certainly highly poetical and seems to some of us to be either mystical or mythical. According to the later Heidegger, the true account is not that man has given birth to language, but rather that man is born out of language.[59] This language is the arrival of Being itself,[60] and it is language itself that speaks rather than man expressing himself in language.[61] "Man is where being's voice is heard and given room. Man is the loudspeaker for the silent tolling of being."[62] So impersonal does this function of language seem to become that one of the new school can claim that what counts in interpreting a text is not what the intention of the author was, but "What shows itself in this text?"[63]

This philosophy is put to the service of religious thought in the doctrine of word-event (Ebeling) or language-event (Fuchs). Fuchs illustrates the meaning of a language-event through the meaning of the word "brother." A man is not my brother because of a biological fact, but he becomes my brother in my naming him so; the "event" of my word to him has an ontological power to constitute him as my brother.[64] Now in analogous fashion the "saving event" is also a "language-event," for true language is God's saving word.[65] This is then linked with the "historic Jesus" who is heard not as "objective factuality" but as "word of address."[66] Further, there is continuity between Jesus' word and the word of the preacher today. Bultmann would separate the kerygma of the early church from the historical Jesus, but the new hermeneutic sees them as belonging together: There is "a recurrent event of language that moves from Jesus' word to that of the preacher."[67]

The thrust of this doctrine is toward a "translation." Early in the essay from which I have drawn this account, Robinson says that the new hermeneutic "does understand its task as translating meaning from one culture to the other, from one situation to the other."[68] So much so that Ebeling is convinced "that theology itself *is* hermeneutic, for it consists in translating what the Bible has to say into the word for today."[69] Thus the *traditum*, what is handed on, must become *traditio*, the act of handing on: "The text fixed in letters becomes the spiritual occurrence of the oral word."[70] And Hans-Georg Gadamer, who after Heidegger is the philosopher of the new theory, agrees that "translation" describes the main thrust of the movement. He adds, however: "But the bold and yet inescapable consequence is that the word has primacy over the text, for the word is language event."[71] In any case, despite return to the biblical call to decision, we are still struggling with the cognitional element that preoccupied Newman and the modernists on the Catholic side.

The concentrated effort in each of these chapters has been to find the transition points and the significant thematizing events that usher in a new stage of history in the theology of the word. These stages may be long or they may be short. The reign of truth lasted a thousand years as a key concept. That of the *loci* lasted some three centuries. In the hundred years since Newman movements have followed one another in rapid succession. But I think it is possible to find a perspective that unites the seemingly disparate activities of a Newman studying historical change, of a modernist striving to adapt the word, of an existential exegete hoping that through the Holy Spirit the word will speak to his self-understanding, and of theologians of the language-event who find the text of scripture interrogating them. Not only that but the same perspective sees the early missionary, the apologist, and the Platonist allegorizer as moving prethematically in the same direction. They are all intent on finding in an ancient word a message and a voice that speak to me today. And that is a theme that reveals the movement of history in the theology of the word, turning us from excessive concern with the past to make us ponder our own situation, the claim the word has on us, and our own response. I do not think any of the movements we have considered has finished the task it set out to accomplish. But they did, all of them, help move us into a new phase, especially the modernists and the hermeneutical efforts of the Protestants. It remains now to see what further themes in these rapidly moving times may bring us a step farther.

CHAPTER SIX

THE PRIMARY WORD: JESUS CHRIST YESTERDAY AND TODAY

With the events described in chapter five we are coming to a major turning point in the theology of the word, comparable in its fundamental significance to the step taken when Saint Paul, or some unknown bearer of the early Christian message, came to realize and boldly declare that message to be the very word of God at work in the believer. This last step, however, is being taken in our own time, so we are working under the disadvantage of trying to write history while we are contemporary with it. Still, fairly clear lines are emerging from this giant stirring; it is possible to see them as continuing the trajectory of previous movements and having their own anticipations far back in history, so we can hope to delineate the new phase at least in some rough manner. The viewpoint remains that of an observer of history, doing theology *in oratione obliqua*, even though, in trying to clarify the obscure beginnings of a new moment, I may seem to take a more personal stand toward particular doctrines.

The situation, then, is as follows: After a long, tranquil, but uncritical period of simple possession of the truth, and a rather long period of reaching back to the word that was the source of the truth, there followed a short period of diverse programs and activities aimed at bringing those ancient sources forward into our own day, as truth relevant for me and a word to me putting a claim on my response. This can be seen as a twofold aim, with one aspect that is cognitional and one that is affective. Correspondingly, the deficiencies in the programs and activities so far studied are twofold: They leave the word an ancient word that does not speak to my situation, and the word becomes objectified in such a way as not to challenge my response. Is the forward movement of history that will remedy these deficiencies also going to be twofold? It is facile to demand a unity on the ground that the history of theology is also part of the divine salvific plan and God's plan must be one and single. But even God judged it wise and good to proceed in two steps: "When the term was completed, God sent his own Son . . . that we might attain the status of sons. To prove that you are sons, God has sent into our hearts the Spirit of his Son" (Gal. 4:4-6). And so I see the present stirring in the theology of the word to have two distinct though closely interrelated aspects, to be studied separately in chapters six and seven.

Cognitionally, then, the efforts examined in chapter five are inadequate. Early efforts to stretch the meaning of a word given in the past, to make it mean what we need it to mean today, have either been discredited or allowed to die a natural death; they did not provide for that control of meaning which scientific exegesis requires. Newman's idea of development may be valid up to a point, but it does not account for all the data. There are surely linear developments; but there is also a dialectical factor, there seem to be quite disconcerting reversals, and there are apparently independent new beginnings, and all these call for a deeper explanation. Even where Newman's idea is valid, we still have to meet the objection with which Chadwick ends his volume on development.

> The question then for those who think Newman's theology is Catholic, is this: these new doctrines, of which the Church had a feeling or inkling but of which she was not conscious—in what meaningful sense may it be asserted that these new doctrines are not "new revelation"?[1]

Modernists might be more open to the dialectic of history, but they did not have an acceptable answer for Chadwick and, worse, did not seem concerned about such a question to the extent demanded by a church that insisted on continuity with the sources.

Efforts on the Protestant side presented their own difficulties. We may be sympathetic to the two conditions Bultmann posits for hearing the ancient word: a common preunderstanding and the work of the Holy Spirit. But the first is made to bear too great a weight: There is the factor of history, which is set aside, and there is the factor of what some call the "strangeness" of the ancient word; both need attention. As for the second condition, theologians cannot admit the action of the Holy Spirit but then simply set him aside as a factor that is incomprehensible; they have to try to see his role in some intelligible relationship to the whole of God's salvific plan. When we turn to the theology of the language-event, we find it too much involved in the obscurities of the remythologizing of the word, too much so for it to satisfy the rigorous demand of the human mind for such understanding as is possible of the divine mysteries— especially when it would neglect the mind of the author of a work in order to invoke some message that is independent of his intention.

Is any clear line of progress in sight? The previous chapter found an opening by reversing the direction of thought: Instead of moving back from the present, as in chapter four, we studied the forward movement from the origins of the word into the present. Can this be invoked in a new way? That is, instead of moving forward from the word of Paul about Jesus, could we go back to the reality of Jesus himself of whom Paul spoke, and then come forward from that new starting point with a new wealth of meaning to be exploited through the centuries? Such approximately is the approach of the new thematization of the Christian word. We go back beyond the Easter word of the apostles to the human reality of Jesus himself, his appearance on earth, his life, death, and glorification in the Easter event, and take that reality as God's most fundamental word, a primary word, an inexhaustible word, one that the church and her spokesmen from Peter and Paul to John tried, more or less adequately, to interpret. Indeed the process of interpretation could go back behind Peter to Jesus himself; and surely it goes forward beyond John to the present day.

A few clarifications may help. The first: I repeat that I am not settling the question of the "historical" Jesus, but simply recording the thought of the early church and of certain theologians on his role. The second: Although I refer to the *human* reality of Jesus, this reality is not circumscribed by some thirty-three years in Palestine. He is God's first creative idea: "In him

everything in heaven and on earth was created" (Col. 1:16). We
might refer to him as the cosmic word, but not just in the Greek
sense of cosmos; that sense must be expanded in two ways: to
take in the whole space-time universe in its four-dimensional
reality, and, much more significantly, to take in the realities
studied by the human sciences. Then maybe Teilhard de Char-
din's view of the place of Christ in the genesis of the universe
could serve as a symbol round which to collect our ideas, but it
seems better to use the terminology of recent thought and take
history as the word of God, history understood with an absolutely comprehensive sweep that embraces the visible universe.
A third clarification: This history is not the history that is written, of which we spoke in our Introduction; it is the history that
happens. It is therefore much wider than the history of the theology of the word, the history to which this book would contribute; for, as utterly comprehensive, it includes the history of
ideas and doctrines as a small part of the whole. Finally, the
reader might keep in mind that, as the missions of Son and Spirit
are closely linked in trinitarian theology, so we expect to find a
link in their respective roles in regard to the word of God; this
chapter should therefore be read with some corrective influence
from anticipation of the chapter that follows it.

1. Prethematic Stage: History and Typology
in Scripture and the Fathers

Our regular procedure of searching the ancient documents
for anticipations of an idea thematized much later yields good
returns here. There are some remarkable hints of our theme in
the scriptures.[2] There is, first of all, an orientation to history as
the place where God acts and reveals what he is. Thus, in the
Old Testament we have assertions to the effect that God covered
himself with glory in the exodus (Ex. 15:1-21), or that he made
his judgment known from heaven in the defeat of the enemy (Ps.
76[75]), or that he will reveal his holiness by his justice (Is. 5:16).
This orientation shows history as a source for our knowledge of
God, though it does not articulate the notion of God's using
history as a medium to speak a word to us. Nor does a series of
passages in the New Testament that continue this way of thinking and show the same orientation. For example: "Christ died

for us while we were yet sinners, and that is God's own proof of his love towards us" (Rom. 5:8). Again, God's "love was disclosed to us in this, that he sent his only Son into the world to bring us life" (1 Jn. 4:9). And the evangelists attribute this mentality to Jesus too: When the Baptist sent to ask whether he is the one who is to come, "Jesus answered, 'Go and tell John what you hear and see . . .' " (Mt. 11:4). As John says, he revealed himself: "This deed at Cana-in-Galilee is the first of the signs by which Jesus revealed his glory" (Jn. 2:11).

However, other New Testament passages seem to take a distinct step forward. The letter to the Hebrews begins:

> When in former times God spoke to our forefathers, he spoke
> in fragmentary and varied fashion through the prophets. But
> in this the final age he has spoken to us in the Son whom he
> has made heir to the whole universe.

There is question here of a word God spoke, and it is related to the prophetic word of the Old Testament, which it completes in final form: The suggestion is that the Son himself, in his very being, is God's new and final word. In any case, that is the conclusion to be drawn from a passage in Paul's second letter to the Corinthians. The context here is trifling, almost puerile. The Corinthians have evidently accused Paul of being fickle in that he changed his purpose of visiting them. Paul rejects the charge, appeals to God's truth as witness, and suddenly breaks forth in this magnificent statement:

> The Son of God, Christ Jesus, proclaimed among you by us
> . . . was never a blend of Yes and No. With him it was, and
> is, Yes. He is the Yes pronounced upon God's promises,
> every one of them (2 Cor. 1:19-20).

The unspoken context in which Paul makes this declaration is a question from Israel and an answer from God. The question: Is God faithful to his promises? The answer: A divine yes, not a yes written with pen and ink in a certain language, or a vibration in the trembling air, but a yes spoken as God alone can speak it, in the very person of his Son whose meaning is: Yes, my people, I, your God, am faithful.

There is another anticipation in early Christian times of the idea that history is a word of God, and it is found in the emergence of typology. The New Testament writings make fairly extensive use of this device, beginning with St. Paul. He speaks of certain Old Testament events as types, or, in the translation of the New English Bible, as symbols, meant to provide a lesson for us: "These events happened as symbols to warn us not to set our desires on evil things" (1 Cor. 10:6). Again, "All these things that happened to them were symbolic, and were recorded for our benefit as a warning. For upon us the fulfillment of the ages has come" (1 Cor. 10:11). The basic meaning seems much the same as in our modern usage, when we speak of "making an example" of some offender, but Paul's use of the basic idea is overlaid by his sense of the whole Old Testament as pointing to "the fulfill-ment of the ages" that has come in Christ. This usage, which naturally goes beyond Philo through its application to the Chris-tian message, runs through the New Testament; with varying nuances it is found in 1 Peter and the Pastorals, in 2 Peter, and very markedly in Hebrews. This letter, using a number of Greek words to convey the same general idea, speaks of the law, cult and sanctuary, gifts and sacrifices, and other institutions of the Old Law, as copies, shadows, symbols, of what is found in the New (8:5; 9:23, 24; 10:1; etc.).[3]

Jean Daniélou has investigated several examples of the pa-tristic use of typology: Adam, Noah and the flood, the sacrifice of Isaac, Moses and the exodus, and other Old Testament figures or events are seen by the fathers as types of Christian realities.[4] Daniélou maintains further that typology is a true sense of scripture, where allegory is not.[5] This brings us very close in-deed to an explicit formulation of the idea to which this chapter is devoted.

2. Thomas Aquinas: Breakthrough without Follow-up

The next significant step is the clear and explicit formulation of the idea implicit in the two sets of data found in scripture and the fathers: that God speaks through the events of history as really and truly as he does through the word of prophet or page of scripture. Apparently this explicit stage was already antici-pated in Junilius, a questor at the court of Justinian,[6] but I am going to leap forward to the Middle Ages and Thomas Aquinas, in whom we find at one and the same time a remarkable clarity in the exposition of the idea and a pronounced reluctance to exploit it in his theology. I believe his exposition has direct relevance to modern discussion of history as revelation, and that the reasons that grounded his reluctance to use the idea extensively no longer apply in the same way; so I regard his contribution as a significant step in the ongoing history of the theology of the word.

The Thomist position and argument are as follows: Scripture comes to us as words chosen by the author to communicate to us the truths necessary for salvation. However, the expression of truth may be achieved in two ways, either by words or by realities (*rebus*); that is, words can refer to realities, but also one reality can refer to another reality. Now it is the special prerogative of scripture, which has God for its author, that both the words of scripture and the realities to which they refer are subject to divine control and therefore to divine use of them as instruments of his meaning. Saint Thomas is shorter on examples than he is on the principle at stake, but he speaks of the Old Law as referring to and signifying the New, the synagogue as signifying the church, the twelve stones taken from the Jordan as signifying the twelve apostles. Thus, the literal meaning of scripture, when it speaks of the Old Law, is just that: the Old Law; but the spiritual meaning, the meaning of the reality referred to, is the New Law.[7]

Clearly, the specific contribution of Saint Thomas to the present question derives from his views on God's use of created realities to manifest his divine meaning, and that in turn is inserted in his larger view of the divine control of all events in the created universe. This latter is a complex question in which "we must have precise ideas . . . on the nature of operation, premotion, application, the certitude of providence, universal instrumentality, and the analogy of operation."[8] On the complexities of this larger question I can only refer the reader to the classic study just quoted, but once that idea of the universal instrumentality of all creation under the operation of God is understood, it can be imported easily enough into the present area. That is, the whole of creation is as much under the dominion of God as pen or voice is under the dominion of human author. Add only the simple notion that the visible universe is as well qualified to be the expression of meaning as are vibrations in the air or ink marks on paper, and you have all the elements you need for the Thomist theory: God writes history by control of events just as men write human language by control of pen, and the resulting "language" of history expresses God's meaning, is God's word to us.

Saint Thomas was cautious almost to the point of being reactionary in the use of this idea. He invoked it only to explain certain instances of typology, and then only because scripture, in declaring specific Old Testament events to be types of the New, forced him to deal with the question. His primary sense of scripture was always the literal: We cannot base any argument on the "spiritual" sense, except, of course, where it is revealed to us later in the literal meaning of a passage. Nor do we need this "spiritual" sense, since anything found in it is also found elsewhere in the literal, if it is necessary for our salvation.

My own concern now is to exploit the Thomist idea for a modern theology of the word of God, and that involves consideration of three points: generalizing Saint Thomas's idea, reversing his priorities in regard to the literal and spiritual senses of scripture, and taking account of the reasons for his reluctance to give the spiritual sense any prominence in his own thought or exegesis. The first point is quite simple: To generalize Saint Thomas is to conceive the whole of history, and not just certain specified events, as a word from God, as "uttered" by him with a meaning for us. And the possibility of such generalization is provided by Saint Thomas himself in his view of God's universal providence and activity: As God governs all history, so obviously he can use all history to convey his meaning. The second point is a little more complex: To reverse the priorities of Saint Thomas is to make the meaning of history primary and the (literal) meaning of scripture derivative, not the other way around. This is not provided for in the Thomist context of thought, but it is not difficult once we accept the modern view of prophecy and sacred writing as interpretations of the world around us and of the events of history. We have only to note that then we consider the universe not merely as possessing intelligibility, as the physicist may do, but also as possessing the meaning proper to language; this the believer who regards it as God's creation may easily do. Briefly, as the human sciences differ from the natural in that for them meaning is a constitutive part of the data, so the universe of the theologian differs from that of the physicist or philosopher in that it is constituted by meaning as well as by physical or metaphysical elements. Furthermore, we may say that this view is not so much *contra* Saint Thomas as it is *praeter* his views. That is, the viewpoint is different; Saint Thomas saw the matter *quoad nos*, and therefore for him scripture was primary, for he saw no way of getting at the meaning of events except through the scriptures that revealed that meaning. But our present viewpoint is that of the *quoad se*, and then there is a case for making history the primary word of God; whether there is any way for us to penetrate to that meaning, except where scripture reveals it, is another question that brings us to our third consideration.

The real question then is why Saint Thomas himself was so cautious in his use of what he called the spiritual sense, the meaning of history. Put more cogently still, the question is why the virtualities in the Thomist idea were not exploited long before this. My general answer would be that on one side there was no pressure to exploit them, and on the other there was the evident danger deriving from the lack of control over meaning in the field of history. Saint Thomas himself would certainly see no necessity for developing the views he had set forth on divine activity in history and divine use of history as a medium for the word. The pressure the allegorizers had once felt, to give an acceptable meaning to the Old Testament, had been reduced with the recognition of the New Testament as the word of God in its own right. The pressure arising from the varieties of culture, the genetic view of history, and the recognition that the biblical mentality differed notably from that of the modern Western world was still in the distant future. For Saint Thomas the word of Paul or John could be transported without difficulty across the centuries; after all, God *was* the principal author of scripture and he did not change with journeys across time and space. In any case causality interested Thomas more than meaning in the universe.

But all this is rather remote from what would prove to be the fundamental question; it explains only why the idea would hardly occur in the first place. More directly, the question for anyone who proposed a view of history as God's fundamental word would be, How do you control the meaning you give to history and to the word of God that you declare it to be? We seem to be back with the airy speculations of the allegorizers, who had no other justification to offer for their interpretation than that it made God more acceptable to the Western mentality. To bring interpretation of God's word in history under control, there was needed both the Thomist view of universal instrumentality, and, besides that, a theory, possible only in our times, of history. Even the Thomist understanding of universal instrumentality was not always understood by his immediate successors, and a theory of history was far in the future. We are coming presently to a discussion of that modern theory, but one very important factor in the theology of the word is intermediate between Saint Thomas and the 20th century. It is the profound conviction expressed in the theology of the spiritual masters that God speaks to the individual believer in the events of his personal life. This is the notion we have next to study.

3. The Spiritual Writers: God's Voice in Every Event

It is remarkable that the inhibitions felt by professional theologians in regard to history as the word of God have been largely ignored by the spiritual writers, who have gone their own quite radical way without, however, falling into the absurd exaggerations of the old allegorizers. Among these spiritual writers Jean Pierre de Caussade, who died at Toulouse in 1751, merits special mention for the clarity of his expression, the really radical nature of his views, and their pertinence to our question. His ideas were not put into book form during his life, but after his death his "treatise" on abandonment to divine providence was put together from his letters of spiritual direction. The context, then, is ascetical practice, and the relevance to the present question lies in his doctrine that the divine will is made known to us in the events of daily life, which speak to us, which are God's word to us, just as really as the words of scripture.

One can recognize the Thomist background of his thought in

his two declarations, "The divine action . . . is everywhere, and always present,"[9] and, "Things, in fact, proceed from the mouth of God like words."[10] But Père de Caussade, the spiritual writer, is far less inhibited in applying the second of these two principles than Saint Thomas, the theologian. For de Caussade, "All has meaning. . . . Not a comma is missing."[11] Thus,

> The written word of God is full of mystery; and no less so His word fulfilled in the events of the world. These are two sealed books, and of both it can be said "the letter killeth". . . . The sacred Scripture is the mysterious utterance of a God yet more mysterious; and the events of the world are the obscure language of this same hidden and unknown God. . . . They are what He has revealed! He has dictated them! And the effect of these terrible mysteries which will continue till the end of time is still the living word, teaching us His wisdom, power, and goodness.[12]

Further, the parallel between scripture and history is carried out thoroughly:

> The Holy Spirit . . . writes His own Gospel in the hearts of the just. . . . The souls of the saints are the paper, the sufferings and actions the ink. The Holy Spirit with the pen of His power writes a living Gospel, but a Gospel that cannot be read until it has left the press of this life, and has been published on the day of eternity.[13]

So emphatic is de Caussade that he almost seems to make the scriptures inferior as a word to the word of history:

> . . . it seems as if Your wonders were finished and nothing remained but to copy Your ancient works, and to quote Your past discourses! And no one sees that Your inexhaustible activity is a source of new thoughts. . . . Is not all time a succession of the effects of the divine operation, working at every instant . . .? . . . May the divine operation of my God be my book, my doctrine, my science.[14]

And, again:

> You speak also to each individual soul by the circumstances occurring at every moment of life. Instead, however, of hearing Your voice in these events . . . men see in them only the

outward aspect . . . and censure everything. They would like to add, or diminish, or reform . . . they respect the holy Scriptures, however, and will not permit the addition of even a single comma. "It is the word of God" say they. . . . All this is perfectly true, but when you read God's word from moment to moment, not written with ink on paper, but on your soul with suffering, and the daily actions that you have to perform, does it not merit some attention on your part?[15]

In the context in which Père de Caussade was working it was right that the doctrine be applied to each individual person: The events of one's personal life are God's word to that person. But it is not so limited in principle: "You speak, Lord, to the generality of men by great public events. . . . You speak also to each individual soul by the circumstances occurring at every moment of life."[16]

The positive side of this remarkable doctrine is surely clear enough by now. It remains that it does not satisfy the theologian's demands for a theology of the word. For one thing it concentrates almost exclusively on the will of God, whereas a theology must say a great deal on the being of God and his work of creation. Again, though it supplies the personal element that Luther and modern Protestant exegetes so earnestly seek, a word of God for me, still it lacks the present surety of public revelation: "The divine action continues to write in the hearts of men the work begun by the Holy Scriptures, but the characters made use of in this writing will not be visible till the day of judgment."[17] Only faith enables us to recognize in history what the apostles recognized on the shore of Galilee after the resurrection: "It is the Lord."[18] From the viewpoint of the ascetic, this deficiency is of little moment; it is enough to know that this moment is from the Lord. Particularly is this true from the viewpoint of de Caussade's favorite doctrine of abandonment to the divine will. It is otherwise for those who have to interpret that divine will as directing us to a specific action. Nevertheless, this doctrine remains an extremely interesting and significant stage in the ongoing history of the theology of the word. I do not know whether its history has been fully investigated in its origins[19] and its subsequent development, but I do think there is need to bring it into relation with that work of professional theologians which forms the bulk of material for our study.

4. Emergence of a Theology of History As Word

Saint Thomas Aquinas formulated a principle that is available to us for a theology of history as God's word, but he did not apply it widely. The spiritual writers applied the principle to every least event in public or private life, but they lacked any means of controlling their interpretation except that supplied by their own piety; this was quite sufficient when it was merely a matter of seeing God's will in every event and accepting it obediently; but it was quite inadequate for any specific interpretation of God's meaning or for any positive action that God might be supposed to be enjoining on the individual person. We are not ready to tackle the question of the individual believer and his "word" received privately and directly from God, but we can move toward a public view of the meaning of history through recent advances.

History was not a prominent category when the rage was for system, but efforts to conceive it are very old and these efforts of millennia are coming to something like a focus in modern views of history.[20] The ancient Greek historians (Herodotus, Thucydides, Polybius) were concerned to rescue history from the low estate to which the philosophers consigned it, and so they looked for the universal in the enormous flow of particulars. When Christianity came on the scene, the concern shifted to discovery of the divine purpose running from Adam to the *parousia*, and Ireneus, Augustine, Joachim of Fiore, Bossuet, would exploit that idea. But a view of the divine purpose and providence was not enough; there was needed a philosophy of history. Unfortunately, philosophy had its own ideas, quite opposed to those of the theologians: The notion of progress took the place of that of providence, and the Christian attention to particular, contingent events was set aside when the Greco-Roman notion returned with a vengeance: Only what is universal is significant. The careful attention to details, which had been the hallmark of the "antiquarians," had to be made respectable again by von Ranke, and Vico had to come along to join philosophy to theology, development to providence, the empirical to the universal. Further, Protestant theology developing from Luther's focus on Christ (his *Sachkritik* of the scriptures in effect would eliminate any books or writings that did not witness to Christ) became sensitive to the idea of salvation-history developed by von Hofmann in the 1800s. Though the separation of history into two departments called sacred and profane is now repudiated, the thrust toward a theological notion of universal history is not.

Wolfhart Pannenberg, in his article "Hermeneutics and Universal History,"[21] relates his position to the existential approach of Bultmann and to the language approach represented by Gadamer. His introductory paragraphs set up the problem: A two fold gulf has opened up in study of the scriptures, one between the text and the events to which they refer, and the other between the texts and our own time; one presents the problem of historical study, the other the problem of hermeneutics. The two are, however, closely related, closer reflection shows their unity, and the question becomes "whether the totality which includes both aspects is to be identified as hermeneutic or as history."[22]

In pursuit of an answer Pannenberg recounts the history of hermeneutics as it runs from Schleiermacher through Dilthey to Bultmann, on the last of whom he concentrates. He finds that both the psychological interpretation of Schleiermacher and Dilthey and the existential interpretation of Bultmann restrict "the question concerning the significance of the past for the present to the question concerning human existence";[23] the content of the text, unintentionally but in fact, is "narrowed down from the outset."[24] Pannenberg would restore the wider view. The New Testament, for example, is concerned "with many things other than possibilities of understanding human existence"; these writings "are concerned also, and indeed in the first instance, with God and his participation in the events of the world and its history."[25] Pannenberg further asks "whether the historical distance between [past and present] is retained in all its profundity if one subordinates the text to an anthropocentric understanding of existence, as do Dilthey and Bultmann."[26] The past must be retained *as past* and, as past, related to the present, and this requires another approach to the problem:

> If the historical distance of that which is past is held on to, then the connection between that which occurred and was formulated in the past, and that which is present, could

hardly be found anywhere else than in the very context of history, which binds what is current to what is past, and in that way the hermeneutical question would be taken up into the universal-historical question.[27]

Pannenberg now turns to Gadamer's views. "The way in which past and present are to be set into an understanding relationship to one another, Gadamer describes excellently as a 'fusing of horizons.' "[28] He goes considerably beyond Dilthey and Bultmann, in Pannenberg's view: (1) He does not relate the text to be understood to a "pre-understanding" in the interpreter; the text is "strange" to the interpreter, who must not conceal its distance from his horizon. (2) He must form "a comprehensive horizon, which embraces the horizon both of the interpreter and of the text, horizons which at first confronted one another as alien."[29] (3) In this way he is "able to go beyond the limits of his original mode of questioning and his preconception"; he is able to do so because his horizon is not rigid but moving.[30]

This project of a comprehensive horizon, says Pannenberg, involves a total understanding of reality and so, in view of the distance separating interpreter and text, takes "the form of a historically differentiated understanding, and thus of an aggregate of historical accommodation on the part of the present."[31] Gadamer does not undertake this total understanding, and in fact repudiates Hegel's attempt to perform a total mediation of past and present; against Hegel Gadamer insists on the openness of experience and of the future, and the finitude of human thinking. How then does Gadamer mediate past and present? By reflecting on the linguisticality of the hermeneutical experience. He uses the model of conversation. The interpreter must find "the question to which the text was an answer," and then this reconstructed question passes over into the question that the tradition represents for us.[32] Pannenberg rejects the analogy of conversation; only by metaphor, he says, can one hold that the text poses a question to us.[33] He also criticizes Gadamer's devaluation of the statement, of the "assertion"; Gadamer insists that every statement has an infinite, unspoken background, to which Pannenberg replies that this does not diminish the value of statement; rather it becomes the interpreter's job to turn that background too into statement.[34]

Pannenberg finds that Gadamer "has his hands full in attempting to keep his thoughts from going in the direction they inherently want to go";[35] "the phenomena which Gadamer describes move time and again in the direction of a universal concept of history, a concept which he would like to avoid in view of the Hegelian system."[36] Pannenberg, in his own position, accepts this thrust:

> If interpretation has to do with the relationship between then and now, so that the difference between them is preserved when the hermeneutical "bridge" is built, and if, further, one must go behind the text by asking about its unspoken horizon of meaning, about its historical situation, so that the first task of the interpreter is to frame the historical horizon from which the text comes, then the only way that the historical situation of the text can be adequately linked to the present time of the interpreter is through an investigation of the historical context of the present in its connection with the situation as it prevailed when the text was written.[37]

Pannenberg agrees, however, with Gadamer's repudiation of Hegel; Gadamer, he says, has formulated the point that separates all contemporary thought from Hegel: "finitude as the vantage point of thinking, and the openness of the future."[38] He himself returns to the conception of universal history. How can one formulate it without closing off the future in a Hegelian manner? By a provisional and proleptic conception, Pannenberg says, accessible already in the history of Jesus and its relation to Israelite-Jewish tradition;[39] "the original eschatological meaning of the history of Jesus" is that of "an anticipation of the end."[40]

Pannenberg's own positive views may be seen in some of his theses on revelation as history, as given in this convenient list:[41]

Thesis 1: The self-revelation of God in the biblical witness is not of a direct type in the sense of a theophany, but is indirect and brought about by means of the historical acts of God.[42]

Thesis 2: Revelation is not comprehended completely in the beginning, but at the end of the revealing history.[43]

Thesis 4: The universal revelation of the deity of God is not yet realized in the history of Israel, but first in the fate of Jesus of Nazareth, insofar as the end of all events is anticipated in his fate.[44]

Thesis 5: The Christ event does not reveal the deity of the
God of Israel as an isolated event, but rather in-
sofar as it is a part of the history of God with
Israel.[45]

Thesis 7: The Word relates itself to revelation as foretelling,
forthtelling, and report.[46]

It is not clear how fully Pannenberg would subscribe to the
view set forth in this chapter, for, although in his explanation of
his seventh thesis he can speak of history as the language of fact,
he seems to maintain a distinction between revelation and the
word.[47] Nevertheless, his views recommend themselves for
their general stance toward history, and for their insistence on
linking the meaning of Christ to the history of Israel and indeed
the whole of history. Furthermore, I find them helpful as a
means of setting this general approach into relation to modern
streams of Protestant thought. Nevertheless, for a theology of
the word that corresponds to this sixth stage of our own ongoing
history, I prefer to take over his general idea without committing
myself to every detail of his exposition, and to formulate it in
what to me are simpler terms more in continuity with Thomas
Aquinas and Jean Pierre de Caussade.

In this view, then, the very realities of creation, seen as a
whole and therefore necessarily incorporating the totality of history, are God's "word" to us in some basic and primary sense.
Then, all prophecy, all our traditions in doctrine, all our
scriptures, are successive attempts, feeble and stammering but
ever so precious, to understand, conceive, formulate, and express the inexhaustible meaning of this primary word. In this
view we take up the Johannine view of "Word" and "witness"
that in chapters two and four we found to go far beyond the
prevalent contemporary view and to anticipate much later developments. But we add to John the history, not perhaps of the
Word, but of the interpretation of the Word. That is, because the
meaning God uttered in his Son and in universal history contains
more than human industry will ever fathom, therefore it can be
seen in one way by Paul, in other ways by Mark, Matthew,
Luke, and John, in still others by the thinkers of the Greco-
Roman world of the fathers, and in quite different ways by
modern 20th-century man. And all these interpretations will be

linked to one another by this at least, that they refer to the one reality that they all attempt in different ways to understand; further links can then be established by the ordinary genetic and dialectical approaches to various interpretations. And this view will see the interpretation that Jesus himself formulated as one in the series; it may even have less interest for Christology insofar as Jesus may be presumed not to have spent his time thinking about himself, but it will have a superlative value for the center of theology, for our views on the great God and his designs for the human race.

This position goes beyond Newman without denying the validity of his basic insight. That is, there may well be virtualities in the "great ideas" of revelation that contain future developments that may unfold without further revelation, but we are not limited to a development that unfolds like the growth of a tree with preservation of type, continuity of principles, logical sequence, and the rest. We have the possibility of going back to the beginning whenever we wish and starting all over again with a new set of great ideas, provided only we have the creative intelligence to grasp and formulate them. Not only that, but we can establish a dialectic between different stages in a stream of thought; logical sequence is no longer a decisive criterion. And nothing impedes a high degree of pluralism in the interpretations, approaches, traditions, sequences of thought.

I should not leave this chapter without noting a structural kinship between the threefold word of Karl Barth and the ideas expressed just now on the primary word of God, the interpretation given that primary word in scripture, and the subsequent reinterpretations given it as the church in the course of time tried to formulate God's message for herself and for those whom she is charged with evangelizing. As Otto Weber describes Barth's doctrine, there is the preached word, which we hear in the church; there is the written word of scripture to which the church must be obedient in her proclamation; and there is the revealed word that "happened" in the incarnation of the Son of God; and here we are "confronted with the 'first' form of God's Word—the form which is determined by nothing outside itself, and which determines all the others."[48]

Nevertheless, when we come to the process by which one

moves from the primary word to the present time, Barth's differences from the views of this chapter become evident. Thus,
speaking of Calvin's work, he says:

> How energetically did the latter, having first established the
> text, then rethink the entire content and explain it, until the
> wall which separated the 1st century from the 16th became
> *transparent*, until St. Paul *speaks* and the man of the 16th
> century hears, until the dialogue between the original docu-
> ment and the reader comes to settle on the *subject matter*, so
> that there is no longer any distinction between then and
> now.[49]

However much one may approve the "rethinking" of the text,
there is here a Kierkegaardian bypassing of history to make the
reader contemporaneous with Christ and the scriptures, which
sets Barth poles apart from the ideas I have tried to outline.

It will help conceive our next chapter more clearly if we
have an accurate idea of exactly what step was taken in the
present one. One question, then, that should be answered is this,
In what way does this view of history go beyond Aquinas and de
Caussade? Does it give a specific meaning to history, or is it just
an empty form? Aquinas could make room for a specific meaning, but was able to find out what it was only through scripture;
de Caussade tended to stop with the empty form, the conviction
of faith *that* God was speaking, without the possibility of learning in this life *what* he was saying. How does our view get beyond that?

I would say that the meaning of the Son is a further dimension of his intelligibility; it is that intelligibility understood not
just as a creation with its inner nature and laws, but understood
as a word that is meant. And that intelligibility is subject to
investigation by the array of sciences that we can invoke but
Saint Thomas could not. Biology, psychology, sociology, politi-
cal science, and the rest—all of them throw light on what Jesus
was and what God means to say to us through and in him. Again,
there are the phenomenological, existentialist, personalist
philosophies that can be brought to bear on the intelligibility of
Jesus and consequently his meaning for us. Third, there are the
new theologies, the theology of work, the theology of the world,

the theology of prayer—they too help interpret the meaning Jesus had for us. All of these together, and others too, can be made tributary to a theology of history in which the meaning of Jesus for the whole space-time universe can be investigated.

But this does not answer our questions on the meaning of Jesus; at best, it holds out hope of reaching an answer. And even when the answers are eventually given, we have by no means come to the end of our ongoing and developing theology of the word. For one thing the array of sciences I have invoked is a far cry from the word of prophet or evangelist. We may think of theology as a whole view, corresponding to history as the whole reality of creation, but such a total view is hardly a word for me in the way Nathan's was for David: "You are the man." A more urgent question is the following: Paul's interpretation of the Christian reality has the guarantee of his charism to inspire us with confidence; so has that of Mark, or Matthew, or Luke, or John. What equivalent can we find in any interpretation of history that may occur to our minds? Have we anything more than a fine theory? Has it any more validity than that of a bright idea? How can we possibly verify it? And, supposing that we can and do verify this view, does it advance us on our way in the religious interpretation of the word? Have we reduced Jesus, as some might claim,[50] to an inert, objectified content that the interpreter may study as passive subject-matter but not encounter as a challenge to his personal involvement? These are some of the questions that lead us to surmise that a further step in the theology of the word is demanded.

CHAPTER SEVEN

THE INNER WORD OF THE SPIRIT

The theology of the word set forth in chapter six needs complementing if it is to understand Jesus to be today what he was to the early believers, one who calls and challenges, and not just an objective figure or doctrine to be studied and discussed. The danger of such a dualism between doctrine and life is real and probably permanent, with an exaggeration in one direction succeeded by an overemphasis in the other, as the church strives to maintain an uneasy balance. Thus, catechism can tend to become a matter of questions and answers, of doctrines to be memorized, with a perpetual need for the catechist to add an awkward appendage stressing the conduct that should correspond. Or, at the opposite pole, there is a jubilant call to togetherness and action, with a lack of clarity on what we are together for and why precisely we are to do what is being advocated.

The division of the Father's one salvific plan into the two missions of Son and Spirit, together with the role we have seen the Son to have as God's primary word to his children, establishes an antecedent probability that the Spirit will supply the complement we are looking for. And, indeed, no matter how much the Christian looks upon the Lord Jesus as God's word, as a fully adequate word calling him to response, he will not wish to deny Paul's complementary doctrine that "no one can say 'Jesus is Lord!' except under the influence of the Holy Spirit" (1 Cor. 12:3). So some duality in the unity of God's plan seems built-in and unavoidable, and the task is seen as a matter, not of denying the efficacy of the word that the Son is, but of asking by what means the word becomes effective, by what channel the word comes through as word to me.

There is more than the clue of a general probability pointing

124

to the Spirit as the one in whom we find the theology of the word centered now. We began with a word that was given in the past. In chapter five we found a new state of the question that regarded the present; it is not enough to have a particular word spoken once upon a time to a particular people in sometimes quite particular circumstances: We need a present word spoken to us in our immediacy. Chapter six did not meet that need directly; it went behind the ancient word as we first conceived it to a reality whose meaning is believed to be relevant today ("Jesus Christ is the same yesterday, today, and for ever," Heb. 13:8), but it did not show us how to bring that word forward into the present. Is it not precisely here that the divine wisdom of the two fold sending becomes operative? The Son came once for all, *ephapax*: "He has appeared once and for all at the climax of history" (Heb. 9:26). But the Spirit is given as often throughout the ages as there are believers to receive him: "I will ask the Father, and he will give you another to be your Advocate, who will be with you for ever" (Jn. 14:16). Since believers do not remain on earth forever, but one generation succeeds another, modern theology understands this word, as Acts shows it being realized, of a continuing Pentecost. The Spirit does not come *ephapax* at all, but over and over as often as anyone believes in Jesus.

Again, we have dealt with the word in a predominantly objective way. We spoke of the gospel, of the gospel as word, of the word as truth, of the truth as grounded in the sources, of the sources as subject to deepening understanding, till we came to the view that what God really said, primarily and fundamentally, he said in his Son, the objective and visible entry of God into the world. For the Son was "born of a woman." He is *par excellence* the objective factor in God's word and revelation; and so faith and theology are at one in rejecting as unbelief every attempt to dispense with the historical Jesus. Still the subjective side kept cropping up all along the way: in the reception of the word by believers, in the charism of the agents of the word, in the certitude of the truth preached and believed, in the credentials of the spokesmen of the word, in the enlightenment with which deeper understanding is achieved. Is it not the Holy Spirit who represents all these aspects, and does this not suggest that a further and complementary chapter is called for on the Spirit to remedy their omission?[1]

There are still other ways the point could be made and the surmise reinforced that we have here a clue to the next stage of history. As object and subject are correlatives, so also the external and the internal are correlatives. Now the external word is visible and palpable, so that John could say: "We have heard it; we have seen it with our own eyes; we looked upon it, and felt it with our own hands; and it is of this we tell. Our theme is the word of life. This life was made visible" (1 Jn. 1:1-2). But the Spirit is internal: "God has sent into our hearts the Spirit of his Son" (Gal. 4:6), and "God's love has flooded our inmost heart through the Holy Spirit he has given us" (Rom. 5:5). And there is a parallel difference between the public and the individual aspects: The word of God came to the herald of Jesus "in the fifteenth year of the Emperor Tiberius, when Pontius Pilate was governor of Judaea, when Herod was prince of Galilee . . . during the high-priesthood of Annas and Caiphas" (Lk. 3:1-2). It was a public act. The Spirit has his public manifestations too, but he is also given inwardly to the individual person, and so "there are varieties of gifts, but the same Spirit. . . . One man, through the Spirit, has the gift of wise speech, while another, by the power of the same Spirit, can put the deepest knowledge into words. Another, by the same Spirit, is granted faith. . . . But all these gifts are the work of one and the same Spirit, distributing them separately to each individual at will" (1 Cor. 12:4-11).

These clues seem worth investigating. I do not propose to study the trinitarian basis of the Son/Spirit complementarity, but simply to investigate how it works out in a theology of the word spoken on earth to the human race. This gives us a number of options that seem pertinent to the respective roles of Son and Spirit: There is in Lonergan's levels of conscious intentionality the complementarity of the third (cognitional) and the fourth (affective); there is that of the ontological and the existential (the modern, not the Thomist existentialism); there is the content of conscious performance and there is the activity; there is orthodoxy and there is orthopraxis; there are the contrasts we have seen of outer and inner, objective and subjective, public and individual. It is probably not of fundamental importance which option is chosen, but only a matter of convenience. I propose then to study the data from the general viewpoint of *interiority*, which stands for the subjective and individual factor that we attributed to the Holy Spirit. As always I begin with the prethematic stages of the doctrine, that are found already in the New Testament, and follow it through history till the question becomes explicitly posed and so representative of the seventh and final period in our history of the theology of the word.

1. Biblical Data on Interiority

The scriptural data on interiority have hardly begun to be investigated, but one very useful study has been done from the viewpoint of a doctrine of spirituality[2] and I will preface my own contribution with a synopsis of that study.

In the Old Testament several terms designate what we would call interiority. There is *nephesh*, translated for want of a better word as "soul." It sometimes stands for the individual person (in English too we say "a hundred souls"), but sometimes it stresses the idea of vitality and then it corresponds to what we would call the subjective pole of experience. A second term, *ruah*, which means wind, breath, or spirit, evolved toward an association with human subjectivity and came to be regarded as the manifestation of interiority, intellectual or affective. But the richest and most versatile of the terms describing interiority in the Old Testament is *leb*, the heart. As the physical organ of the emotions, it naturally became the symbol of what was most intimate to a man; however, we should note that for the Orientals it was not just the organ of love but also that of thought and intellectual activity. *Basar*, the flesh, also had a part in the personal and spiritual life, and other terms (reins, bowels, etc.) served as metaphors for interiority.

In the New Testament Saint Paul offers a complex set of anthropological terms. He adds two typical Greek words, *nous* (intelligence) and *syneidêsis* (conscience), to his theological vocabulary, both offering data for interiority, but he uses soul and heart in the traditional way of the Hebrew scriptures. However, heart becomes important for present purposes in that "It is by the heart or in the heart that the believer receives and locates interiorly *(intériorise)* the gifts of God: faith, charity, and the

Holy Spirit in person."[3] As for *nous* and *pneuma* (spirit), Saint
Paul differentiates them "as two distinct accounts of the same
spiritual life, the one of clear thought linked to language, and the
other of direct experience of God" that can remain unobjec-
tified.[4] Finally, there are three occurrences in Paul's letters (or
the Pauline literature) of the synthetic expression "interior
man": Romans, 7:22; 2 Corinthians, 4:16; Ephesians, 3:16.

The synoptic gospels show Jesus adding new images that
evoke interiority. One image is that of the treasure, as when the
good man is said to produce good things from the good treasure
of his heart (Mt. 12:35; Lk. 6:45). Another is that of the good
ground that receives the word (Mt. 13:23). There is the image of
the eye that discerns the good (Mt. 6:22-23), and that of the
"secret" hidden deep in man to be seen by God alone (Mt. 6:4, 6,
18). Jesus also, according to the synoptics, contrasts inner and
outer and applies the distinction to man (Mt. 7:15; 23:25, 27, 28;
Lk. 11:39-40). The significance of this will depend very much on
the theory one adopts of the interiority of Jesus. Finally, John's
gospel provides data for interiority in terms of reciprocity and
dwelling in one another: God dwells in us and we in Christ (6:56;
15:5,7) through love (14:20; 17:22-23). His first letter adds specific notions to this mutual indwelling: The word of God dwells in
us too, as does his witness, and the anointing we have received
from him (2:14; 5:10; 2:27).

Let us turn from language to performance where, perhaps, I
can make a more specific contribution. We will be examining,
then, the elements of interiority that are revealed, not by words
like heart and soul, but by the activities described in the
scriptures. This is a very large question, but one can usefully
indicate the direction of research to be undertaken, and give
some account of the materials to be studied.

First and most obvious are the operations of conscious intentionality recorded in the scriptures. They are myriad but with
the help of a basic structure we can bring the multiplicity into
some order. That structure, as was partially indicated in chapters three and five, is established by the set of basic questions.
There are questions for intelligence: "How can this be?" (Lk.
1:34); there are questions for reflection: "Are you the one who is
to come . . .?" (Mt. 11:3); and there are questions for delibera-

tion: "Then what are we to do?" (Lk. 3:10).[5] What these questions reveal is an operational structure in the biblical writers
parallel to that which we discover in ourselves, and even in
scientists and philosophers. The difference in materials is vast,
but it should not mislead us, or cause us to overlook the similarity in performance.[6]

A second field for investigation is also obvious but not quite
so amenable to structuring: It is that of feelings. Paul practically
wears his heart on his sleeve, but the synoptic writers too, despite their remarkably objective approach, occasionally allow
their own feelings to show through; one suspects, at least, that
there is a great depth of repressed feeling in the account of Peter's denial of the Lord: "Peter remembered how Jesus had said
to him, 'Before the cock crows twice you will disown me three
times.' And he burst into tears" (Mk. 14:72). In John we are
dealing again with a man whose deep feelings show on nearly
every page. Moreover, the New Testament, in the gospels, of
course, but in the letters too when the occasion offers, presents
Jesus as a man of deep feeling: for those in mourning and need,
for the crowds who are like sheep without a shepherd, for little
children, for sinners and outcasts, for his own disciples; and not
only for others, but in the face of his own trials: He was a man
who was afraid, who struggled with his own call from the Father.

A third area is more difficult. It has to do with a derivative of
the structured set of operations in man, with patterns of consciousness that become established, with stages of meaning that
are reached as a people evolves, and the like. Let me illustrate.
A first example: We distinguish with ease between dreams and
waking experience; so in general did the biblical writers. But this
distinction is not an original given, nor was it achieved automatically; at some point in history it was articulated and became part
of the cultural heritage of the people. When did this happen and
how? A second: The mentality disclosed by phrases like "supposing that," or "as if," or "contrary to fact," or "of course," and
dozens of others—such a mentality is already highly developed;
again, the development was not given, and it did not occur automatically; when did it take place and how? A third set of examples might be the assumptions people take for granted and again
the assumptions they are beginning to criticize. What I am sug-

gesting is that these examples point to a study of the incipient objectification of interiority, and to the stages in its history. I do not know of any study of this question as it pertains to the scriptures, or of any history of the question in general. But it is obviously of great importance for an investigation of interiority.

The fourth area is still more difficult: the area of religious interiority in those who speak the word of God. It would be linked, in its generalities, with the questions raised in the three preceding areas, but would add very important specifications. There is a body of empirical data to be collected. For example, when Jeremiah says: "Oh, the writhing of my bowels and the throbbing of my heart! I cannot keep silence" (4:19), he is surely revealing to us something of the prophet's interiority. But I think that a more important set of data is to be found in a subtler investigation, that of the inner authority with which a prophet or evangelist, or spokesman for God in general, speaks or writes. We could bring the question into focus in this way: Does Mark, or Matthew, or Luke, or John, have to ask anyone to underwrite his account of the gospel? Is there any sign at all in Mark or the others of anything less than total conviction? of relying on views that they do not quite trust, that may turn out to be fallacious? There is surely an authority in the way they speak and write that reveals something of the interiority of the gift that was theirs.

That brings us, of course, to Jesus himself as he was seen by early believers, and to the authority with which he spoke. He too was a prophet, he was *the* prophet, and he was more than a prophet:

> Jesus did not expound Scripture academically like the Rabb. He spoke to the people with God-given directness and power as the OT prophets had done. . . . Hence the people said that "he taught them as one having authority, and not as the scribes," Mt. 7:29. . . . The distinction between Him and the Rabb. was not one of degree as between different teachers. It was a fundamental one. He taught as one especially authorised by God, so that His Word was God's Word which men could not evade. The term *exousia* is not used of the work of the OT prophets. But it expresses in the Gospels something similar to the "Thus saith Yahweh" of the OT. . . .

> Yet the superiority of Jesus to the OT prophets is continually stressed. . . . Jesus is not to be set alongside the OT proph-

ets. He is the One who brings the new age which the OT
prophets had only foretold. . . . Jesus is not just a prophet;
He is the One who fulfils the prophecies.[7]

The same thing applies to a comparison of Jesus with Moses. If
the gospels show him as a second Moses, they at the same time
show him as more than a Moses:

> The power and authority of the eschatological prophet may
> be seen in the "I say unto you" as contrasted with the "thou
> shalt" of Moses, Mt. 5:22. . . . Jesus as prophet is not just
> God's mouthpiece. . . . His *ego̱ de lego̱ humin* sets him
> directly at the side of God.[8]

What is a man who is more than a prophet and more than a
Moses? And what can we surmise about his interiority? From
what hidden source does he speak and teach and give com-
mands?

The synoptic answer to this question, or rather the synoptic
remarks from which we might derive an answer, center on the
role of the Spirit in the life and activity of Jesus. It is clear that
the Spirit works in what we could call the consciousness of
Jesus. Thus Mark in his blunt way tells us: "Thereupon the Spirit
sent him away into the wilderness" (1:12). Matthew thinks of a
gentler influence: "Jesus was then led away by the Spirit into the
wilderness" (4:1). Luke is closer to Matthew but adds here and
elsewhere a remarkable doctrine of the role of the Spirit in the
life of Jesus: "Full of the Holy Spirit, Jesus returned from the
Jordan, and for forty days was led by the Spirit up and down the
wilderness" (4:1). He has Jesus begin his mission to the public,
"armed with the power of the Spirit" (4:14), and in his sermon in
his hometown of Nazareth has him quote Isaiah: "The spirit of
the Lord is upon me" (4:18). The great hymn of jubilation begins:
"At that moment Jesus exulted in the Holy Spirit" (10:21).

John, however, is not content with a doctrine that sees
Jesus receiving the impulse of the Holy Spirit from time to time,
or even with a view that sees Jesus in permanent possession of
the Spirit. He goes considerably beyond such thinking to attribute to Jesus, as something that belongs to him in his own right
as Son, an inner knowledge or source of knowledge that is not
restricted. He presents Jesus indeed as one who does not need

information from anyone on earth: "He needed no evidence from others about a man, for he himself could tell what was in a man" (2:25; see 6:64); as one who brought his knowledge with him from a homeland elsewhere: "He who comes from heaven bears witness to what he has seen and heard" (3:32; see 8:38, 40); and so the disciples in due course are able to say: "We are certain now that you know everything" (16:30).

Later, much later, the scholastic theologians will develop a theology of the vision of God that Jesus had in his human mind. Still later, there will be a school of spirituality to cultivate a special devotion to the interiority of Jesus. But these are distant developments. Avoiding anachronism, we will say merely that with the close of the gospels there is at hand material on which to build a reasonably solid structure of doctrine on the interiority of Jesus, as it was glimpsed by the early believers.

2. Augustine, Aquinas, and Interiority

Research and interpretation are needed as much for the subsequent history of interiority as they are for the scriptural period, so it is difficult to seize upon the major turning points and discover what was going forward. But it is possible to isolate some elements of a history, and one of these would surely be the medieval scholastic view of human interiority. It derives from Aristotle in part, but in a more significant way from Augustine, who is commonly regarded as the Christian master of interiority, and it comes close to systematic expression in Aquinas.

Augustine had been preceded in Greek philosophy by Socrates with his precept "Know thyself."[9] But Augustine was "the first great philosopher of interiority."[10] In him the Christian message of interiority found its first extensive elaboration, with the incorporation also of Greek anticipations. He was, he tells us in his *Confessions*, "a question to myself." His program was to know himself and God. To achieve wisdom was to achieve knowledge of one's inmost self: "Noli foras ire, in te ipsum redi, in interiore homine habitat veritas." In Saint Augustine, interiority is not just a way of philosophizing; it is also a psychological reality, and a philosophical principle with metaphysical consequences. "Interiority is self-consciousness."[11]

The complex intermingling of streams and variety of approaches evoked by the names of Aristotle, Augustine, and Aquinas have been analyzed as follows:[12] Aristotle had a metaphysics of "soul." Though he practiced introspection he did not thematize it, and so, where "the Platonic *nauta in navi* is suggestive of the subject, the Aristotelian soul is not. It is an inner principle, constituent of life. It is defined as the first act of an organic body. It is found in all organic bodies, in plants no less than in animals and men."[13] Augustine, however, with a different personal background, arrived at a different view of interiority; he was "a convert from nature to spirit; a person that, by God's grace, made himself what he was; a subject that may be studied but, most of all, must be encountered in the outpouring of his self-revelation and self-communication."[14] So the object of study for him is not the Aristotelian *anima*, differentiated by potencies, with potencies known by acts, acts specified by objects, and objects defined in terms of causality; rather, it is the *mens* known by introspection:

> When conscious acts are studied by introspection, one discovers not only the acts and their intentional terms, but also the intending subject, and there arises the problem of the relation of subject to soul, of the Augustinian *mens* or *animus* to the Aristotelian *anima*.[15]

Aquinas needed Aristotle to work out his conception of theology as a science, but he also needed Augustine, the "Father of the West," to ensure that his theology was the expression of a traditional faith. So he adapted Aristotle and refined Augustine's account of interior process to express his own trinitarian theology, without, however, working out the methodological implications of what he had done.[16] And, like Aristotle before him, he practiced introspection without thematizing it.[17] "Thomist thought on *verbum* is metaphysical by its insertion in an Aristotelian framework, and it is psychological in virtue of its derivation from Augustinian trinitarian theory."[18]

This account, set forth in the context of trinitarian theology, I find extremely helpful to locate the thought of Aquinas on interiority in the great streams forming medieval views.[19] Moreover, it is possible to fill in some details of this Thomist thought. The obvious source is the *Prima secundae*, with its analysis of human activity. There are, Saint Thomas says, intrinsic principles of human acts—they are the potencies and habits; and there are external principles.[20] The external principles are again twofold, one inclining us to evil—this is the devil; and one inclining us to good, and this is God, "who both instructs us through law, and assists us through grace."[21] We should note, however, that the new law, though coming from an external source, becomes an interior principle in the sense in which we are now using the word, for "the new law is first and foremost (*principaliter*) the very grace of the Holy Spirit which is given to those who believe in Christ." And so it is an interior principle impressed on the heart, rather than an exterior law written in words on paper.[22]

Another and very remarkable aspect of the Thomist view on interiority has to do with the sources of knowledge. For Saint Thomas they are two fold: "an extrinsic origin on the level of sense, but an intrinsic origin in the light of our intellects." In fact, in the light of agent intellect "the whole of science virtually is ours from the start." To quote Saint Thomas's Latin: "in lumine intellectus agentis nobis est quodammodo omnis scientia originaliter indita."[23] This is the Thomist background for Lonergan's work on the notion of being, the dynamic notion that is an anticipation of all that is, but that again is taking us ahead of the course of history.

Our theme is interiority, and in particular interiority in contrast to external objective principles. Still more precisely, interiority as a factor in the word of God. It is just here that the Thomist doctrine of the light internal to man becomes most relevant. We saw that both the instruction of the law and the assistance of grace were regarded as extrinsic in the sense that they came to man from the outside. But we also saw that the new law as identified with grace becomes an internal principle, further that the light of intellect is an original internal principle of knowledge given with the natural constitution of man. Now Saint Thomas links this natural light with the light that is given by God in faith, and the light given in prophecy.[24] We cannot say that he worked out a theory of a word that is heard from God in the heart, still less a relationship between such an inner word and an outer word heard in the reading of scripture or in preaching. But it does not seem exaggerated to say that he left important elements behind him for constructing a theory along those lines.

3. Religious Experience and Interiority

Interiority is made known to us by way of experience, specifically, inner experience as contrasted with outer experience, the inner experience that we have come to name consciousness.[25] An account of religious interiority must therefore include a description of religious experience and its relevance to a history of the theology of the word. It may seem remarkable at first sight that religious thinking should have glimpsed the notion of interiority before coming to thematize the experience that reveals the interior; however, that seems to have been the sequence, to the extent, at least, that the scriptures contrast the inner man with the outer, but in regard to experience are content to list the various elements of inner experience without proceeding to the genus itself.

Nevertheless, the two aspects are so closely linked as to make it difficult to separate them even within the confines of the same chapter. Everything we saw in the first section of this chapter on the inner man of scripture might very well come under the present section of religious experience. Similarly, the work of Augustine, the first philosopher of interiority, hovers over his own religious experience as over a sort of mirror in which every doctrine he treated finds a manifestation. The long tradition of spiritual writers also combines the two aspects; thus, Thomas à Kempis, who made so much of the inner man, is likewise famous for the sentiment that would rather feel compunction than be able to define it.[26] And so, just as our chapter six had an important phase developed by the spiritual writers, so has our chapter seven.[27] Finally, even the sober, rational, and extremely objective Aquinas has a doctrine of knowledge (i.e., judgment) "per modum inclinationis"[28] that links interior sources of knowledge with an experience that we would now name "apprehension of value."

Literature on religious experience grows steadily, but much of it is not especially helpful for the functional specialty of history. Catholic writers tend to be polemical in their attitude: They are anxious to vindicate the rights of reason against subjectivism, or they see in Lutheranism the forerunner of quietism, or they find the reformers too preoccupied with questions like the certitude of salvation—but none of these interests is central to my study. Protestant writers too can be quite polemical on the topic; and, even when they are more favorable, the lack of a clearly conceived theory makes the work of interpretation inconclusive.

However, it is in Protestant theology that one can find the general lines of historical development. Luther's stress on the passive side of faith led him to rely more on the inner feelings than on outer works for his assurance of salvation, just as faith itself was more a trust in God than an adherence to objective dogmas. Calvin followed this direction, and took up and wrestled with the problem Luther himself had, of giving some critical value to this internal witness. Scholastic tendencies in later Protestant theology would back away somewhat from the individualism implicit in their beginnings, and begin to form a church dogma; but then various movements on the Catholic side would be accused of Protestant leanings: those associated with the names of Baius, Jansenius, Quesnel, and even Pascal, as well as the quietist movement. Pascal would define faith quite simply: "Voilà ce qu'est la foi: Dieu sensible au coeur." But a year later he would modify this to read: "Voilà ce que c'est que la foi *parfaite*: Dieu sensible au coeur."[29]

It was Schleiermacher, the father of modern Protestant theology, who was also the central figure in the development of a theology based on religious experience. He was the heir of pietist, romantic, and sentimentalist influences, as well as of the philosophy of Kant who had done so much to center German philosophical thought on the subject and his interior rather than on the object. For Schleiermacher the essence of religion is in feeling. It is an experience, an immediate sense of our dependence in regard to the universe. Traditional notions of miracles, prophecy, revelation, the supernatural, become transposed in this perspective, and all dogma becomes a construct based on the original data of experience and religious feeling. Before Schleiermacher, our interpreter tells us, there had been an appeal to internal witness (though it still had something of a rational character), but only for purposes of apologetics; after him, this subjective experience became the original datum of faith and the source of dogma.[30]

Various tendencies, by way of development or by way of reaction, followed Schleiermacher. Some would try to give an objective basis to religious experience; others, anxious to retain scripture as the supreme norm of faith, would react against experience: It could serve, as witness of the Spirit, only to illuminate the scriptures. Ritschl established the distinction between judgments of fact and judgments of value, and separated the latter quite rigorously from the former. Thus religion became totally divorced from philosophy. It also became divorced from history, though one could still appeal to the scriptures by distinguishing between the foundation of the faith, which is the person of Christ, and the content of the faith, which is the judgment of value that the human spirit formulated; the latter has nothing to do with the vulgar ways of historical criticism.[31]

4. The Inner Word of the Spirit

From the main stream of theology represented by Schleiermacher and Ritschl in the 19th century, we turn to two currents that at first sight seem rather out of touch with things, and find in them the 20th-century follow-up on interiority. Kierkegaard, who by reason of his belated influence belongs rather to our century than to his own, provides in his definition of truth an entry to his interest in—should we say obsession with?—interiority: "*An objective uncertainty held fast in an appropriation-process of the most passionate inwardness is the truth*, the highest truth attainable for an *existing* individual."[32] If I locate Kierkegaard in my history more as an evangelizer of a new approach than as a philosopher of its theory, this is certainly not to belittle the stature of his thought, but only to turn for theory to another movement where I find it more carefully worked out. That other movement began with the revival of Thomism, but it shifted soon to a transcendental method in which a Thomist structure of cognitional process is fertilized by methodical procedures deriving, with corrections, from Kantian philosophy.

Modern philosophy, from Descartes through British empiri-

cism and Kant to Hegel, has been occupied with a shift away
from concern with the objective world, the grades of being in the
hierarchy of mineral, vegetable, animal, and human kingdoms,
toward a concern with the subject, the human spirit. True, the
subject looks upon this objective world, studies it, organizes it in
science and conquers it in technology. But it has been felt, and
freely admitted by adherents of different branches of this
philosophy, that the trend headed for and ended in a disastrous
idealism, a subjectivism that removed all objective criteria for
judgment on the universe or for evaluation of its possibilities.

At this point the new Catholic philosophy, while not content
merely to revert to the 13th century but anxious to incorporate
the gains of the intervening period, stood its ground and
achieved its own quite different updating. The creative origins of
the movement are attributed to Maréchal, who has found followers in many nations and issued in many systems, but the one
most familiar to me is the philosophy of Lonergan and, since this
philosophy has been put to the service of a basic method in
theology very relevant to a theology of the word, I will limit my
study to an exposition based on his views.

The Thomist universe, as described already, was hierarchi-
cally organized in grades of being, with each being in the material universe itself a composite of the metaphysical elements:
potency, form, and act of existence. Lonergan had no quarrel
with this structure, but he was concerned to give it a critical
basis and methodical foundation. This he achieved by developing Thomist work on the operations of the human subject in the
direction of psychology and introspection, rather than in the
direction of metaphysics. The result—a structured dynamism
issuing in operations on four levels of conscious intentionality:
experience, understanding, judgment, decision.[33] This account
of interiority founded an epistemology, itself in continuity with
elements of epistemology in Aquinas,[34] and metaphysics would
now be a third element in the philosophy, instead of being the
first. It is a philosophy that takes a firm stand against the critical
idealism of Kant and the absolute idealism of Hegel.[35] But it also
recognizes scholastic neglect of the human subject and the need
of a philosophy of interiority, as well as of a critical stance
toward the subject and his cognitional apparatus.

There is much more than modern philosophy in the influences that led to the thinking exemplified in Lonergan's approach and his contribution to a new theology. The other influences are not as easy to document as the philosophical; studies are needed of the influence of Schleiermacher himself, of Kierkegaard, and of others.[36] But the end product in Lonergan can be delineated. The trend was clear by the time he delivered his paper "Theology in Its New Context" at the Canadian Centennial Congress in 1967.[37] There he showed how theology, from being a deductive had become largely an empirical science. Moreover, there is a shift to interior foundations. Theology is now understood as reflection on religion, and fundamental to religious living is conversion. "It follows that reflection on conversion can supply theology with its foundation and, indeed, with a foundation that is concrete, dynamic, personal, communal, and historical."[38] The position is set forth more fully in the work that followed a few years later, *Method in Theology*, and we may turn to that for further details.

For Lonergan, then, as he states his position in *Method*, the primary fact in religion is the gift of God's love: "Being in love with God is the basic fulfilment of our conscious intentionality" (105).[39] It brings joy and peace, it bears fruit in love of neighbor, its absence leads to the trivialization of life, to harshness, to despair. It is a conscious experience of mystery, attractive and fascinating, *mysterium fascinans*, but also *tremendum*, evoking awe in the one who experiences it (105-106).

Religious experience manifests itself. There is a spontaneous manifestation in changed attitudes, the harvest of the Spirit. But there is a more deliberate expression: "It also is concerned with its base and focus in the *mysterium fascinans et tremendum*, and the expression of this concern varies greatly as one moves from earlier to later stages of meaning" (108). This is immediately explained:

> In the earliest stage, expression results from insight into sensible presentations and representations. There easily is pointed out the spatial but not the temporal, the specific but not the generic, the external but not the internal, the human but not the divine. Only in so far as the temporal, generic, internal, divine can somehow be associated with . . . the

spatial, specific, external, human, can an insight be had and expression result. So it is by associating religious experience with its outward occasion that the experience becomes expressed and thereby something determinate and distinct for human consciousness (*ibid.*).

Thus there arise, through the various hierophanies and their multitude, distinction, and forms of unity, the polytheism of a family of gods, the god of this or that place, the god of this or that person, the god(s) of the group (*ibid.*).

In this field of religious expression the spoken and written word find their place as an expression of more than ordinary importance. There are various forms of the word, understood generically: "By the word is meant any expression of religious meaning or of religious value" (112). Carriers of the word or expression are likewise various: intersubjectivity, art, symbol, the lives and deeds of persons. But, "since language is the vehicle in which meaning becomes most fully articulated, the spoken and written word are of special importance in the development and the clarification of religion" (*ibid.*). This "outer"[40] word is not to be regarded as something merely incidental to religion; on the contrary, it has a constitutive role to play. For love that is not avowed "has not reached the point of self-surrender and self-donation"; this holds true for the love of man and woman, and it holds true "in its own way for the love of God and man" (113).

This is not the place to study the function of the word, as Lonergan sees it, in relation to the world mediated by meaning and regulated by value, or to distinguish its personal, social, and historical aspects, or to explore its diversities as it moves through the different stages of meaning, or even to relate it to the doctrines of the church that receives and hands on the word (112, 113-114, 118-119, and see ch. 12). All of that seems to belong, not so much to an ongoing history of questions and ideas, as to a systematic exposition of a particular set of doctrines.

However, there is one further dimension of the word of religion, as it is described in *Method*, that is pertinent here: The specific difference between the Christian word and the word that is simply the expression of one's interiority. This difference is located in the personal entry of God himself into history, "the advent of God's word into the world of religious expression." Other dimensions of the word are, or can be, common to the world religions; but here we come to the distinctive feature of the religion of Israel and the Christians:

> Then not only the inner word that is God's gift of his love but also the outer word of the religious tradition comes from God. God's gift of his love is matched by his command to love unrestrictedly, with all one's heart and all one's soul and all one's mind and all one's strength. The narrative of religious origins is the narrative of God's encounter with his people. Religious effort towards authenticity . . . become[s] an apostolate. . . . Finally, the word of religious expression is not just the objectification of the gift of God's love; in a privileged area it also is specific meaning, the word of God himself (119).

We cannot say that we have here, even in outline, a theology of the word. *Method* is not a theology, but preliminary to a theology, and so this concept of the word is preliminary to a theology of the word. Still the concept can serve to indicate the transition points of history: specifically, in this chapter, to discover what might be the question and idea leading us forward from the position reached in chapter six. I suggest therefore something like the following sequence of ideas: That word which history is, the word that reaches its fullness in Jesus, the word spoken in a language that is God's alone, this word is translated into human language through the pondering and reflection of prophet, evangelist, sacred writer, Jesus himself. As the history is God's word, so any authentic interpretation given by God's agents and with his assistance is also God's word in that secondary but very essential sense described. But the guarantee of authentic interpretation, the source of divine assistance at least to prophet and evangelist, is the Holy Spirit present interiorly, distributing his gifts to each individual at will (1 Cor. 12:11), and likewise distributing the charism of prophecy or inspiration.

There is nothing especially novel or difficult about this idea. There are problems, of course, in its systematic exposition (how, for example, are we to trace the psychological course of inspiration from Holy Spirit to ink marks on paper?), but they pertain to another task of theology than the present. For some, it will be a difficulty that when we have God speaking twice in this fashion, we are introducing an artificial and disruptive duality into the simplicity of the divine revealing activity. But, once we see that two fold activity in God's word as related to the two fold sending of Son and Spirit, the difficulty dissolves into no more than a mode of the mystery of the Incarnation and Pentecost. The Son was sent to be the cosmic Christ, in whom all creation, all history is held together (Col. 1:15-18). The Spirit's relation to the mind of Jesus may be a problem, but he had dwelt in the hearts of the prophets and will dwell in the hearts of Jesus' disciples, to guide them to a true and salvific interpretation of this cosmic history, including their own part in it. If that is distressing to theologians, then they should tackle the problem at its source, and ask why God should send both Son and Spirit in the first place, rather than asking why he found it necessary to speak a radical word in history and use human agents, guided by the Spirit, to interpret it in the course of the centuries.

There are two ways of being one-sided in our approach to this question. The older way showed a concern with the need for the Spirit: If the Son is Savior, what need have we of more? The newer form, put with a similar one-sidedness, would ask about the need of the Son: If the Spirit is the gift of God to all his children, and a sufficient gift for salvation, what need have we of the Son? But the proper form of the question does not start with either one or the other, to ask then about a second sending; instead it tries to conceive God's plan as he himself must be presumed to have conceived it, primarily in its unity. Then the two sendings are joined in the unity of a response to a single need, and the two forms of God's word in the unity of one communication.

Here my history of reflection on the word of God pauses for a while, till the present has turned into the past and we can add new developments. Though its purpose was not to propose for adoption any systematic understanding of the notion, it may nevertheless help toward that end; for what this history presents is the series of efforts to understand and one may expect that, as the series proceeded, it incorporated greater and greater ranges of data and ordered them into a more and more coherent unity. I think personally that in the developments of the last century or so we have the elements for a rather fundamental understanding of the word of God. But that is another story; here it was enough just to recount the history, as I saw it, of reflection on the word. That history has seen many changes. The questions we raise today could not possibly have been raised by Newman or Melchior Cano or John or Luke or Paul. Still there is a continuity that binds us all: There are the same real events described in a way that leads us all beyond the description to the reality; there is one space-time continuum into which both the events and our reflections are inserted, the same Spirit who draws us all to the wonder of those events, the same stirring of mind and heart that links question to question in the genetic sequence I have tried to describe.

CONCLUSION AND PROJECTIONS

My conclusion to these seven chapters will take the form of a simple summary of results, as follows: There is the original situation in which the Christian word is thought of, not yet as the word of God, but simply as a message of good news, essentially a saving narrative to be related, heard, accepted, and handed on. A significant transition, the first in our series, was the recognition that this good news is the word of God in the technical sense which that phrase had for the Jewish people. Next came the transition to the theme of truth: This word of God, "alive and active," cutting "more keenly than any two-edged sword" (Heb. 4:12), was certainly not restricted in its content to bare truth in propositional form; nevertheless, it contained truth that could be cast in the form of propositions, and the second key development was the effort to crystallize the original message in just such a way. But once the focus is on truth you sooner or later realize the need to assign grounds for it, and so the third transition launched the church into the period of concern with the sources of doctrine, the *loci* of theology. *Loci*, however, lie in the past, whereas we live in the present and experience the need to make that ancient word a word for us in our time; that felt need effected the fourth transition in our history: the shift to developing understanding of the word, and its application to present situations. But a word that is thus brought up-to-date is in some sense a new word; the question then arises whether it is still the original word that God spoke to his people; and so in a fifth transition Christian thinkers were forced back to their origins again, to discover there that the real word of God, his primary word, consists simply in the events of his four-dimensional space-time universe with the incarnate Son at its center; and this primary word is subject to ever new interpretations as new questions are put to it in the unrolling centuries. Finally, there emerged as a question the condition of possibility for making that primary word present as the word of God here and now; and an answer is suggested in the way the Holy Spirit inhabits the hearts of believers through all space and all time, enabling them both to receive the word and to hand it on, to understand it and to apply it, and in the original case to be God's agent in giving it human expression.

The pattern shows a chronological sequence. I have put the transition to full recognition that the good news is the word of God in the period ending approximately with Luke's Acts of the Apostles. The transition to the theme of truth I have located in the time of the rise of the councils, the concern with *loci* I put in the 16th century, and the focus on present application of the ancient word in the last century, roughly from about Newman's time to ours. The next stage, reconceiving the original word in its objective moment as simply the divinely governed course of events in the universe with its center in Jesus, was thematized clearly only in the recent past; and the conception of the Holy Spirit as the interior complement to the outer word that the Son is, though it had forerunners at the Reformation, seems only now to be emerging in that precise form.

The transitions are not breaks in continuity, for there is an intelligible sequence as well as a chronological. The force at work in every step is the religiously questioning and reflective power of the human spirit; though the questions are sometimes more explicit and sometimes much less so, they succeed one another in an intelligible pattern: The answer to one prepares the way for another; they are linked together in a structured sequence. Of course, the "structure" is also a "construction" of the historian, his "organization" of history. The role of this organization should be conceived accurately: It is not a matter of inventing data, or of inventing their meaning, or even of inventing the sequence and relationship of document to document and meaning to meaning. But on the other hand our "path" through history is not something given in the way a hidden path is given that we stumble upon in the forest; the elements of data and meaning are just more items lost in an impossible multiplicity, and the course of events is unknown to the participants until the significance of key transition-events suggests itself to the mind as a structuring idea. Then there remains the exercise of critical judgment: not only, Is this a possible way to conceive the pattern and sequence? but also, Was this the actual sequence, or, at least, *an* actual sequence? and, if so, Is the structuring significant enough? Does it organize the data in a sufficiently comprehensive way for the present purpose?

The transitions that articulated the pattern are forward movements, but not just that. There is a sequence, but a linear image is inadequate to describe the complex movement of thought. With each new stage we return to the point of origin, only to move forward again in a wider sweep. Developments in the realm of theology maintain a contact with their past in a way the secular sciences do not. The church finds, as each new question takes her back to her origins, that her history and tradition contain hitherto unthematized riches, untapped deposits. A notion was existentially operative, and the return makes it a theme. For example, the use of *loci* can be discerned in the New Testament writings, and discussion of the reality (without the term) entered Christian theology with Ireneus and Tertullian, but the clear thematization of this idea did not occur till the 16th century when theologians began to write treatises *de locis theologicis*. And so it is with the other themes of our history.

The judgments of my last paragraph begin to look very much like judgments of faith and doctrines of a church, so I take occasion to repeat that history, as conceived here, does not take a stand on the content of doctrines reported on; its stand is simply to state what happened, or probably happened; it is part of theology *in oratione obliqua*: what Paul said, what John said, what relation there is between the two. It was a deliberate decision, therefore, to restrict my conclusion to a mere summary of results, without commitment to any doctrine discussed and without the further steps that might follow such a commitment. I am not, for example, in the preceding paragraph, proclaiming the inexhaustible riches of the word of God; however much I may personally believe in that doctrine, my intention here has been simply to study the way the Christian community has reflected on the matter and to see whether a pattern can be discerned in the ongoing reflection. No doubt my beliefs, as well as my theological preferences, are apparent at many points; but I hope that my sevenfold thesis, separated from the circumstance of its being uttered by a believer, is conceivable, and perhaps even acceptable in principle, for a neutral observer of history. It is through the next functional specialty of dialectic that neutrality is transcended, and this brings us to tasks for the future and some projections.

There are, first of all, tasks that look back from history to research and interpretation. There is, of course, the dependence I have exploited, of history on the two prior specialties; but there is also a reciprocal influence: History raises questions that direct us back to research and interpretation for a fresh investigation from new perspectives. For one example, a great deal has been written on the concept of "witness," its Old Testament and Judaic background, its use in the early Christian community, the implications of that use for our time; but the perspective of our present study raises a question about a marked differentiation of the use of "witness" within the New Testament, and a further question on the degree to which later New Testament usage anticipates a mentality that achieved sharp differentiation and concentrated attention only much later than the New Testament. Again, our history locates Ireneus and Tertullian in a movement coming to explicit formulation long centuries afterwards, and this perspective suggests a reconsideration of their contribution in the light of what can now be seen to have been going forward; it is not a matter of using them to settle a 16th-century controversy—the question is rather: Does the subsequent clarity of the *loci* question give us new insight into the direction of a course of events in which Ireneus and Tertullian were agents though they could not know what was going forward? Similarly, we would reread the early councils from this new perspective, to ask how truth as a theme was differentiated for the assembled bishops within the context of Christian living; we would look in Luther for what evidence there might be in him of an anticipation of the distance between past sources of truth and their present application; and so on.

But the main tasks set by history are discovered, not by looking backward, but by looking forward to dialectic and to the four specialties of a committed theologian, and so we would be moved into the field of values and of the conflicts that are based on fundamental differences of horizon among theologians. Values did not enter history as it was envisaged here; they pose distinct questions with quite distinct criteria required for an answer. Such questions as these: What is the need of religious man for a word? specifically, for a word as contrasted with other forms of religious expression? if it comes to that, what is his religious need for expressions at all? And this sort of question could be raised in every chapter; for example, What is the religious need for truth? what is the value implicitly intended in the practice of "proving" the faith? etc.

The question of values leads inevitably to that of differences and conflicts, since different peoples find different values in the same institution or word. We have, it is true, been concerned with differences, but they were genetic: One question is raised today and receives its answer, only to have a new question raised tomorrow on that basis, and this question must have its own quite different answer. Dialectic is concerned with differences that are different from these. For example: It was enough for me in this study to find a common if unacknowledged purpose in the efforts that ran from the allegorizers through Newman and the modernists to the existential interpretation of Bultmann and to the new hermeneutics of the post-Bultmannians (ch. 5). That common purpose was sufficient to throw some rather deep-rooted differences into the margin and unite the series of thinkers within a single perspective. But suppose we now bring the differences back from the margin into the center of inquiry and begin to investigate their roots. Then we would find profoundly differing views on the notion of interpretation and history, differing philosophies, differing faith-commitments even. Are those differences to be traced to differing horizons? If so, can one describe those horizons for the modern reader in such a way as to provide him with clear options? can one challenge him with a methodically presented option, and through personal encounter draw him to decision and commitment? That is the sort of task that dialectic envisages, and only with its fulfillment would we be ready to tackle the four further tasks of the committed theologian.

These projections amount to saying how little I have tried to do in this book. But if, as Lonergan maintains and I am increasingly convinced, we need "a complete restructuring of Catholic theology,"[1] then our first step is to realize the magnitude of the task before us, and our second is to begin, with what resources we have, to do what is possible here and now. When you have a mountain to move, and only a spade and wheelbarrow to work with, you can either sit on your hands or you can put spade to earth and move the first sod. Some day, if others have the same idea, the mountain will be moved—and restructured. Some day too, I hope, theology will be restructured according to a method that operates on the level of our times; this book is meant to be a spadeful of earth in the moving of that mountain.

APPENDIX

POSSIBILITIES OF METHODICAL COLLABORATION

The urgent procedural problem of theology in our day is that of collaboration. A Saint Thomas Aquinas is no longer possible, and even he in his time depended on the collaboration of his fellows in a way that is easily overlooked. But now the proliferation of sciences and methods, of specialties within specialties, of fields of data divided off and parceled out, all this has forced inescapably upon our attention the necessity of specializing. And if the specialization is not to result in a mere expanding universe of the sciences, in which the galaxies travel farther and farther apart, then there must be collaboration that is methodically conceived and controlled. That is what Lonergan's *Method in Theology* is all about, and it is *Method* that I have tried to implement in this book, as my Introduction explained.

In this Appendix I wish to return to the question and to investigate some possibilities of collaboration, but in an order the inverse of that which governed chapters one to seven. There I drew on the research, interpretation, and detailed historical work of others, scholars in their respective fields. Here I would illustrate a reciprocal influence, from the side of general ideas, on the work of scholars. It is a matter of the function a concept may fulfil in suggesting fruitful lines for particular investigation. In my Introduction I pointed to performance as offering data that are not included in content and might be missed in studies of language and thought-patterns. In my Conclusion I gave some indications of the way history could exercise a reciprocal influence on the very specialties on which it drew for its own task. But in chapter one I proposed a general concept as a scheme for organizing elements in the word of God and its communication; I return to that concept now to study new possibilities latent in its use, enlisting at the same time some help from the other two ideas just mentioned.

There was nothing creative about the use of the concept of communications in chapter one; it served to organize the materials in a sketchy inventory, and had no other merit than that of convenience. But our interest now is in the fertile influence such a concept might exercise in the field of scholarship. Even if it is foreign to that field as a content and as a way of thinking, it may still have a creative heuristic power, a capacity to generate questions, to expand the relevance of ideas, to call up instances of them in the data, to unfold in new ideas that bear in their train their own set of questions and illuminating instances. I will try to illustrate this, but I intend this Appendix less as a test case than as an invitation to scholars to set up their own test case. By that I mean that only scholars can assess the particular results of the experiment, and so I invite them, if they find my illustrations less than stimulating, not to abandon the procedure but to substitute their own more reliable and convincing experiment.

Assume, then, the categories of communication and begin with that of content. We have mentioned the debates of scholars on the primary content, conceived as kerygma, and the subsequent content conceived as teaching. A first step beyond this might be to make more explicit a means to illustrate this double content, the very procedures of the New Testament. Thus, we have Luke's striking procedure of having an audience put the ethical question in almost identical terms early in his gospel and early in Acts. John the Baptist, after delivering his message, was asked, "Then what are we to do?" (Lk. 3:10; see vv. 12, 14); and Peter and the apostles in a parallel situation were asked, "Friends, what are we to do?" (Acts 2:37). Now can we invoke the heuristic function of a concept to take us further still? The later Heidegger and his students speak of objectifying and nonobjectifying thought (I would prefer the word "operations" since thought is of its nature objectifying), and Lonergan speaks of sciences of the object (physics, chemistry, etc.) and sciences of objectification (logic, epistemology, etc.). This suggests to me that we conceive the act of the high priest in tearing his robes (Mk. 14:63) as an objectification, and ask what is being objectified. Similarly, the autobiographical reflections that pervade

Paul's letters, for example, in 1 Thessalonians, from 2:17 to 3:13, may be conceived as a process of objectification, and the same question asked. Do such questions enlarge our views on the content of the message?

Another line of thought is suggested by C. Larcher in an article on the Old Testament word of God, in which he first speaks of the essential content of the revelation-word, derived from the events of Hebrew history, and then goes on to study what he calls "Prolongements et extensions de la parole-Révélation." Such prolongations he finds in institutions and their accompanying traditions of a national or religious or cultic nature: the royalty itself, the rites and ceremonies in local sanctuaries and, later, in the temple. With the appearance of the sacred writings, these prolongations are found especially in the work of the Deuteronomist, the prophetic message of Second-Isaiah, and the transformation of the word accomplished in the sapiential literature.[1] Such a list suggests, partly by way of similarity, partly by way of contrast, a large area for investigation in regard to the Christian message: its new relation to human institutions, national and multinational, social and cultural; those relating to languages, customs and manners, natural science and proverbial wisdom; its new ceremonial and liturgy, etc.

Let us turn from content to agents of the word. In chapter one we drew up a list of those whose "office" in New Testament times might pertain in greater or lesser degree to the communication of the word. If we invoke now the heuristic function of the general concept, the first effect might be to put the question more sharply in regard to marginal cases such as leaders of the assembly and administrators: To what extent, and in what precise way, do they contribute to the transmission of the Christian word? But the next effect will be to raise the question about other categories altogether. For example, the women who provided for Jesus and the Twelve "out of their own resources" (Lk. 8:3), did they not fulfil a function parallel to that of the deacons who undertook their office so that the Twelve might carry on "the ministry of the Word" (Acts 6:4)? and, if so, is their contribution not pertinent to a full description of communication? And what of those who gave hospitality to the apostles or to the local congregation at worship? or of the general class of "patrons" of the message, patrons in the sense that they built synagogues or otherwise gave of their wealth for the sake of the message old or new? Again, we may ask in what sense the "group" in general is expressly or existentially the bearer of the message. Studies being made today of the "social inspiration" of the scriptures give special point to an examination under this heading of the Sanhedrin, the Twelve, the local congregation, the "council" at Jerusalem, the family, even the "two or three" gathered together in the name of Jesus (Mt. 18:20).

In regard to the activities of those who bore the message, a first question again might ask to what extent and in what way the exercise of these various "offices" enters a theology of the word. But the question of extending the list arises here too. For example, "singer" does not seem to be regarded as an office, but the activity of singing was not only a part of worship for Jesus and his disciples (Mt. 26:30) but seems linked closely with the word as well: "Speak to one another in psalms, hymns, and songs" (Eph. 5:19). This suggests renewed examination of liturgical gestures for a theology of the word, for the disciples on the way to Emmaus recognized Jesus at the breaking of the bread (Lk. 24:31, 35). It suggests also investigation of a less familiar area. Today we attach great importance to rapport between persons, and we have Newman's motto expressing this relationship in terms of communication: *Cor ad cor loquitur*; are there instances of such communication in the scriptures? This question leads to another category, which may be called simply "presence." It was important to Paul: "For I long to see you; I want to bring you some spiritual gift . . . to be among you to receive encouragement myself" (Rom. 1:11-12). Thus we might be brought to study the theological significance of a "visit" (1 Thess. 1:9, *eisodos*), and then to put a general question on travel as a category in the communication of the message. Paul's journeys are a familiar topic, to be sure, but I have not seen them treated under this heading.

The use already made of modern categories to raise questions about New Testament activities might be prolonged: The *disputatio* was a famous exercise in medieval theology, and Luke records a fair amount of disputing, proving, challenging in New Testament times (v.g., Acts 9:22, 29); but has this been fully exploited for a theology of the word? Again, the *Spiritual Exercises* of St. Ignatius Loyola are not only a new *genus litterarium* in themselves, but offer distinct possibilities for a more comprehensive theology of the word; do they also suggest new possibilities for research and interpretation in New Testament writings? Other activities are suggested by modern experience: consultation, "rapping," confessor-penitent dialogue, and the like. But the virtualities of a heuristic structure may be even better indicated by a step in the opposite direction. Opposed to speaking there is silence; what can a theory of communication learn from a study of silence? There are the recorded silences of Jesus and others (v.g., Mk. 14:61). But there are also the silences discovered only in the procedures of the New Testament writers. There is the intermediate procedure of the way the four evangelists draw our attention away more and more from the baptism of Jesus by John. What relation have these facts to a theology of the word?

The media of communication are so closely connected with the activities of those who bear the message that the preceding paragraphs have already been a discussion of the media too. But the matter is worth discussing under a separate heading, if only to generalize the question and lift ourselves out of the ruts of the scripture/tradition controversy in which the "word and writing" pair of chapter one tends to become fixed. Begin with a simple practice like almsgiving. Paul himself made a great deal of this as a Christian exercise, but, obviously embarrassed at "talking money," he built up a considerable theology in support of his pleas (see 2 Cor. 8-9). That theology comes close to making almsgiving a medium of the word when he relates it to confessing the gospel of Christ (2 Cor. 9:13), but perhaps the general thrust of his apostolate is more important than the phrases he uses in regard to alms. For example, he thought of his own conduct as a way of teaching, just as Christ's conduct before him was a way of teaching (1 Cor. 11:1; see 1 Thess. 1:6, and 1 Pet. 2:21). Then the author of the Pastorals will link the suffering endured by Timothy and by Jesus Christ to the notion of witness (1 Tim. 6:12-13). What we are coming to, in fact, is the statement that a man's life is the medium of his message, or perhaps the message itself, and so Luke wrote of "all that Jesus did and taught" (Acts

1:1). But, because a man's life is an expression of what he is, we are forced back to his being and character, in the sense in which Paul wrote: "That is the kind of men we were at Thessalonica, and it was for your sake" (1 Thess. 1:5). Here we are on the threshold of important themes of modern hermeneutics; certainly we are liberated from the constriction of the word/writing pair.

Another heading overlaps several subdivisions in our conceptual scheme: that of the agent's conscious, reflective attitude toward what he is doing, toward the recipients of his message, toward his own involvement with them, etc. Take the data on a writer's advertence to his activity. Paul and Luke are explicitly conscious of being engaged in writing, revealing this fact sometimes in phrases that are theologically innocent (1 Cor. 16:3), sometimes in phrases of great theological significance (1 Cor. 14:37; Lk. 1:1-4). But at the other end of the scale we are reduced to what is implicit in the procedures: Mark, for example, hardly lets us know that he is conscious of being a writer; it is merely implied (if the phrase is Mark's) in the words "let the reader understand" (13:14). Then there are data that show an author's awareness of his readers' needs, as when he translates foreign words for their benefit. There are data that show a writer aware of his here and now, as when he says, "This story . . . is current . . . to this day" (Mt. 28:15). There are data that show, less expressly, an author in a running engagement with his adversaries, or in steady progress toward a fixed purpose. Finally that purpose is pursued with a conviction, an assurance, an authority that lead us to ask an old question, but perhaps with new possibilities of an answer based on empirical data: What consciousness, however vague, has a sacred author of a superior power at work in him?

Besides giving there is receiving; besides the *paradidonai* of the one handing on, there is the *lambanein* of the hearer of the message. The two verbs are closely linked correlatives in New Testament thought and in its Hebrew antecedents. Headings can be drawn up here to correspond roughly with those on the side of the agent. For content, there are the credal elements of the New Testament. Corresponding to handing on the message in words, there is the procedure of memorizing on the part of hearers, though it is not clear how large a role this played. Corresponding to the concern of the apostle there is the filial devotion of his congregation. One could complete the list and then invoke the heuristic power of the concept to suggest creative expansion of the various ideas. But perhaps the procedure is becoming tedious, and one example will do to round off discussion: To expand the notion of the agent's activities, I suggested the category of presence, with prolongations in the idea of visiting, traveling, etc. What would the counterpart be on the side of the hearers of the word? For a start, presence would be mutual; but then we might think of prolongations in the notion of expectation (Jewish expectation in regard to God, Corinthian expectation in regard to Paul), perhaps also in that of hospitality, and that of support of the minister of the word. The possibilities for a revitalized theology seem as extensive here as for other headings in the communication of the word.

ABBREVIATIONS USED IN THE NOTES

ACW: *Ancient Christian Writers. The Works of the Fathers in Translation* (Westminster: The Newman Bookshop, 1946-).

ANCL: *Ante-Nicene Christian Library* (Edinburgh: T. & T. Clark, 1867-).

IDB: *The Interpreter's Dictionary of the Bible* (New York: Abingdon, 1962).

LF: *A Library of Fathers of the Holy Catholic Church Anterior to the Division of the East and West* (Oxford: J.H. Parker, 1838-).

ODCC: *The Oxford Dictionary of the Christian Church*, ed. by F.L. Cross, 1st ed. (London: Oxford University Press, 1958).

TDNT: *Theological Dictionary of the New Testament*, ed. by Gerhard Kittel, trans. by G.W. Bromiley (Grand Rapids, Mich.: Eerdmans, 1964-).

TWBB: *A Theological Word Book of the Bible*, ed. by Alan Richardson (London: SCM, 1957).

NOTES

Introduction

1. Scripture is regularly quoted from The New English Bible (NEB). This translation may add too much interpretation to serve the purpose of research or exegesis; but, for history as it is conceived here (presently to be explained in the text), that is a positive advantage.

2. Thus, it is one thing to study the content of the biblical notion of "truth" as revealed in the use of the term itself; it is another to study the activity of questioning, challenging, contradicting, arguing, proving (all these may occur without being named as I have named them), which correspond to our own activities and may reveal a mind in search of truth in the Western and modern sense of the term. This distinction between activity and content corresponds, roughly but usefully, to the scholastic distinction between *actus exercitus* and *actus signatus*, and to the existentialist distinction between the *vécu* and the *thématique*; I have studied its application to the scriptures a little more extensively in my article "Neither Jew nor Greek but One Human Nature and Operation in All," *Philippine Studies* 13 (1965): 546-71.

3. Bernard Lonergan, *Method in Theology* (London: Darton, Longman & Todd, 1972; New York: Seabury). The second edition, 1973, is unchanged except for the correction of misprints. This work will be referred to simply as *Method*, and page references will regularly be given in the text rather than in the footnotes.

4. A key distinction here is that between historical experience and historical knowledge, on which see *Method*, ch. 8, no. 2. This distinction depends in turn on Lonergan's general cognitional theory of the transition from experience through understanding to knowledge, on which see his *Insight: A Study of Human Understanding* (London: Longmans, Green and Co., 1957).

5. The reader will notice a difference between the conception of history I use here and that set forth in Lonergan's *Method*. In the latter work, history is the product of scholarship in the precise sense defined by Lonergan, "a commonsense grasp of the commonsense thought, speech, action of distant places and/or times" (p. 233). Now an overall view such as I have attempted cannot be a work of scholarship in that sense; it is impossible to deploy the needed expertise on every writer, from Paul to Pannenberg, whose work is relevant to the history of the Christian word. But Lonergan's earlier work provided a pattern for such an overall history; see his ideas on the movement of thought, *De Deo Trino*, Vol. 2 (Rome: Gregorian University Press, 1964), pp. 33-53. The notion of history in *Method* does not invalidate this earlier conception, but rather needs it to span the centuries and link stage to stage of development.

Chapter One

1. Rudolf Bultmann, *Theology of the New Testament*, trans. by Kendrick Grobel, Vol. 1 (London: SCM, 1952).
2. My procedure is parallel to that of Hans Conzelmann, *The Theology of St. Luke*, trans. by Geoffrey Buswell (London: Faber and Faber, 1960), p. 207, where he gives as his headings: "the Church as the transmitter of the message, the messengers and their message, their manner of transmission, and finally the recipient of the message and his problems." The use of some such framework is surely standard procedure; it is less common to advert to its heuristic potential; on this see my Appendix, Possibilities of Methodical Collaboration.
3. Charles H. Dodd, *Gospel and Law: The Relation of Faith and Ethics in Early Christianity* (New York: Columbia University Press, 1951), pp. 8-14. See Robert C. Worley, *Preaching and Teaching in the Earliest Church* (Philadelphia: Westminster Press, 1967), for an account of Dodd's development on this point, the criticisms against him, and Worley's own position.
4. There is a question on the means used in Judaism to assure the accuracy and continuity of tradition. Harald Riesenfeld, *The Gospel Tradition and its Beginnings* (London: Mowbray, 1957), thinks of formal memorizing as an important factor; his peers, however, find his position somewhat exaggerated.
5. Under *alpha* alone in a New Testament concordance I found by rough count about 170 relevant words.
6. For example, there is the topic studied for centuries under the name of divine grace. When and where, and with what consequences, did the materials in question receive this name? One distinct act of thematizing took place when Augustine began to write expressly *De gratia*; the consequences are well known: the extraordinary development of the theology of grace, the proliferation of questions analyzing the theme with ever-deeper penetration. But at the same time there was a corresponding loss in breadth: To speak of the grace of God, and to concentrate on the gift as gift, is to shift to the margins of thought many aspects in the living reality that was thus thematized. The theme takes over once it is selected and specified.

Similarly, to give Father, Son, and Spirit the name "Trinity" and to begin to write treatises *De Trinitate*, marks a particular thematizing of certain materials. That thematizing gave an extraordinary impetus to thought on the status of the Son and the Spirit, on the relations of the "Three" (as they had now come to be known) to one another, and on the character of the Community that God is. But it was a particular thematizing, and there was a corresponding loss: Attention was diverted from the work of Son and Spirit in the world; we are only now trying to repair the loss under the heading of the economic Trinity.
7. The count is rough; I have not taken note of textual variants and interpretative difficulties. Ephesians, Hebrews, and the Pastoral Letters are not included in Paul's works.
8. Gerhard Friedrich, *TDNT*, Vol. 3, 1965, p. 704, in the article on *kêryx* and its cognates; the noun can also mean the act of proclamation (p. 716), but the importance of the content should not be overlooked (p. 710).

9. Gerhard Friedrich (using notes of J. Schniewind), *TDNT*, Vol. 2, 1964, p. 708, in the article on *euaggelizomai* and its cognates.

10. Charles H. Dodd, *According to the Scriptures: The Sub-structure of New Testament Theology* (Fontana book from the 1952 original; London: Collins, 1965). See also his pamphlet *The Old Testament in the New*, Facet Books: Biblical Series, No. 3 (Philadelphia: Fortress Press, 1963; republished from the 1952 original).

11. Conzelmann, *op. cit.*, p. 218.

12. Charles H. Dodd in *The Ministry of the Word*, ed. by Paulinus Milner (London: Burns and Oates, 1967), p. 45; Dodd's contribution to the collection is "The 'Message' in the Gospels and Epistles," pp. 45-64.

Chapter Two

1. H.H. Rowley, *The Faith of Israel: Aspects of Old Testament Thought* (London: SCM, 1956), ch. 1.

2. Otto Procksch, *TDNT*, Vol. 4, 1967, p. 94, in the article on *legô*, Part C: The Word of God in the Old Testament.

3. A. Robert, *Supplément à la Dictionnaire de la Bible*, ed. by L. Pirot, A. Robert, and H. Cazelles, Vol. 5 (Paris: Letouzey, 1957), col. 443, in the article on *Logos*, Part II: La parole divine dans l'Ancien Testament.

4. Georges Auzou, *The Word of God*, trans. by Josefa Thornton (St. Louis: Herder, 1960), p. 37.

5. J.N. Sanders, "Word, The," *IDB*, Vol. 4, 1962, p. 870.

6. Auzou, *op. cit.*, pp. 35-39.

7. C.H. Dodd, *The Authority of the Bible* (Fontana book, revised edition of the 1929 original; London: Collins, 1960), p. 151.

8. C.H. Dodd, *The Parables of the Kingdom* (Fontana book, revised edition of the 1935 original; London: Collins, 1961), pp. 14-15.

9. Joachim Jeremias, *The Parables of Jesus*, trans. by S.H. Hooke (London: SCM, 1954), p. 61.

10. Is there a similar contrast in John between *rêmata* (which he uses only in the plural) and *logos*? Cf. 12:48, "There is a judge for the man who . . . does not accept my words (*rêmata*); the word (*logos*) that I spoke will be his judge on the last day." But *rêmata* too has a profound depth of meaning: "He whom God sends utters the words (*rêmata*) of God" (3:34).

11. Gerhard Kittel, *TDNT*, Vol. 4, 1967, p. 120, in the article on *legô*, Part D: Word and Speech in the New Testament.

12. *Ibid.*, p. 126.

13. Hans von Campenhausen, *The Formation of the Christian Bible*, trans. by J.A. Baker (Philadelphia: Fortress Press, 1972), p. 178.

14. *Ibid.*, p. 102.

15. *Ibid.*, p. 80.

16. *Ibid.*, pp. 148-165.

17. *Ibid.*, p. 186.

18. *Ibid.*, p. 188.

19. *Ibid.*, pp. 262-268.

20. Kittel, *op. cit.* (n. 11 supra), p. 125.

21. Dodd, *op. cit.* (n. 7 supra), chs. 2-3.

22. M.H. Shepherd, Jr., "Prophet in the NT," *IDB*, Vol. 3, 1962, p. 919.
23. *Ibid.*, p. 920.
24. Alan Richardson, "Inspire, Inspiration," *TWBB*, p. 114.
25. *Ibid.*, p. 920.
26. Robert M. Grant, *A Short History of the Interpretation of the Bible*, rev. ed. (New York: Macmillan, 1963), p. 18.
27. *Embassy for the Christians*, trans. by J.H. Crehan. *ACW*, Vol. 23, 1956, p. 39 (in no. 9; and see no. 7, p. 37).
28. Campenhausen, *op. cit.* (n. 13 supra), p. 279, n. 68.
29. *Ibid.*, pp. 316-317.
30. J.Y. Campbell, "Word," *TWBB*, p. 284.
31. Kittel, *op. cit.* (n. 11 supra), pp. 117f.
32. *Ibid.*, pp. 118f.

Chapter Three

1. This catalogue of possibilities is taken from an unpublished paper of Bernard Lonergan, *De argumento theologico ex sacra scriptura*, written for a faculty seminar at the Gregorian University, Rome, 1962; the list is applied directly to scripture, and the concluding possibility is that scripture may be considered as the word of God, not to be contradicted. The list appears in a somewhat modified form in Lonergan's mimeographed notes, *De methodo theologiae* (lectures at the same university), 1962, p. 54; there it applies directly to the word.
2. The polemics for and against dogmas make it difficult to write a history that prescinds from values, but it ought to be a factual question whether a dogma is "catholic" in the sense referred to. See Lonergan's discussion of the Athanasian understanding of the consubstantiality of Father and Son, *De Deo Trino*, Vol. 1 (Rome: Gregorian University Press, 1964), pp. 23, 48, 54, 75, 85, 107, 131, 140-141, 142-143, 202. A similar point is made about the "minimal" character of conciliar dogmas, *De methodo theologiae* (n. 1 supra), p. 57.

An extensive study of the relation Lonergan sees, in the middle period of his career, between scripture and dogma is that of Quentin Quesnell, "Theological Method on the Scripture as Source," *Foundations of Theology: Papers from the International Lonergan Congress 1970*, ed. by Philip McShane (Dublin: Gill and Macmillan, 1971), pp. 162-193, with numerous valuable notes, pp. 245-254.
3. Again we have to avoid being drawn by polemics into discussions of the value of truth. For some theologians "the facts about Jesus" (Acts 18:25; see 1 Cor. 15:3-8) offer a sorry message of salvation; see André Malet, *The Thought of Rudolf Bultmann*, trans. by Richard Strachan (Shannon: Irish University Press, 1969), pp. 154-165, 185-197. But we could not discuss this with Malet without going deeply, as he does, into highly theoretical questions on the nature of truth, objectivity, and the like. From my viewpoint these questions should be left, as far as possible, to a later functional specialty. I find it helpful to study the role of the question in the emergence of the truth-function of the word, but the basic and quite sufficient meaning of

162   THEOLOGY OF THE CHRISTIAN WORD

truth itself is contained in the plain and obvious sense of "yes" and "no," of "is" and "is not." We may say, technically, that these words are existential in the Thomist sense (pertaining to the existing universe) rather than in the sense of modern existentialist philosophy. Now Bultmann himself acknowledges this "objectifying" trend in the scriptures; it is a weakness, indeed, says Bultmann, one to which even the great Paul succumbed in his treatment of the resurrection (Malet, pp. 157-158); however, it is there, and that is enough for my present purpose.

4. E.C. Blackman, "Truth," *TWBB*, p. 269.

5. R. Bultmann, *TDNT*, Vol. 1, 1964, pp. 241-247, in the article on *alêtheia*, Part D: The Early Christian Use of *alêtheia*.

6. Bernard Lonergan, *Insight: A Study of Human Understanding* (London: Longmans, Green and Co., 1957), pp. 271-272.

7. This paragraph just touches a very large topic, which I cannot develop. But let me mention a few headings. There is a series of *meta* compounds that deal with distorting the gospel, turning away or being dislodged from it (Gal. 1:6, 7; Col. 1:23; see also 1 Cor. 15:58). There is a variety of other metaphors: falling, being tossed about by gusts of teaching, being seduced and carried away; and their opposites: standing, remaining, being fortified, etc. There is the permanence of truth based on what is solid rock, firm foundations, and ultimately on the unchanging character and security of God. So the prophecies "must" (*dei*) be fulfilled.

8. A pertinent and useful study here is that of Vernon H. Neufeld, *The Earliest Christian Confessions* (Grand Rapids, Mich.: Eerdmans, 1963): It centers on the *homologia*.

9. *Trallians*, trans. by James A. Kleist. *ACW*, Vol. 1, 1949, no. 9, p. 77.

10. *Magnesians, ibid.*, no. 11, pp. 72-73.

11. *The Epistle(s) of Saint Polycarp . . . to the Philippians*, trans. by James A. Kleist. *ACW*, Vol. 6, 1948, The Second Epistle, no. 7, p. 79.

12. *Fragment 2*, trans. by James A. Kleist, *ibid.*, p. 115.

13. *Proof of the Apostolic Preaching*, trans. by Joseph P. Smith, *ACW*, Vol. 3, 1952, no. 3, p. 49.

14. Walter Bauer, *Orthodoxy and Heresy in Earliest Christianity*, trans. by a team from the Philadelphia Seminar on Christian Origins (Philadelphia: Fortress Press, 1971), p. xxiii. Origen is quoted from his *Commentary on the Song of Songs*, 3.

15. *Ibid.*, p. xxi.

16. The word occurs in his "Cognitional Structure" in *Collection* (New York: Herder and Herder, 1967), p. 229: "So the question, What's this?, promotes the datum of sense to a 'this' that has a 'what-ness' and 'is' " (see also p. 236). Lonergan uses it regularly thereafter.

17. J. de Ghellinck, *Patristique et moyen âge: Etudes d'histoire littéraire et doctrinale*. Vol. 1: *Les Recherches sur les origines du symbole des apôtres* (Gembloux: Duculot, 1946), pp. 18-20.

18. De Ghellinck, *op. cit.* (n. 17 supra), traces the fascinating history of these researches.

19. See A.E. Burn, *An Introduction to the Creeds and to the Te Deum* (London: Methuen, 1899), pp. 282-286, on *tessera* and *symbolum*. But J.N.D. Kelly, *Early Christian Creeds* (London: Longmans, Green and Co., 1950), pp. 52-61, gives a more nuanced account with reservations on some of Burn's points.

20. See Denzinger-Schönmetzer, *Enchiridion symbolorum definitionum et declarationum de rebus fidei et morum*, 33rd ed. (Barcelona & Freiburg [Breisgau]: Herder, 1965), nos. 125-126.

21. *Ibid.*, no. 3011.

22. The formulation is that of G.L. Prestige, *God in Patristic Thought* (London: S.P.C.K., 1952), p. 213.

23. *Method*, p. 179, and see the Introduction supra, pp. 3-4.

24. The pattern is not rigid; for example, "anathema sit" does not always denote a dogmatic definition of faith, and so there is need of interpretation. See Piet Fransen, "Réflexions sur l'anathème au Concile de Trente . . .," *Ephemerides theologicae lovanienses* 29 (1953): 657-672. Also it may simplify history to speak of Nicea as setting the pattern; there were earlier, if less successful, conciliar efforts to bring truth into focus.

25. *On First Principles*, trans. by G.W. Butterworth (New York: Harper Torchbooks, 1966), Bk. 1, Preface no. 3, p. 2.

26. Migne, *Patrologia latina*, Vol. 34, col. 547: "nonnulla enim pars inventionis est, nosse quid quaeras."

27. *Ibid.*, Vol. 178, col. 1349: "Dubitando enim ad inquisitionem venimus; inquirendo veritatem percipimus." Abelard does not simply assume one side is right and the other wrong; he gives a list of means for reconciling apparently contradictory statements and only when they have failed does he resort to judgment on his authorities: "conferendae sunt auctoritates, et quae potioris est testimonii et majoris confirmationis, potissimum retinenda" (col. 1345).

Chapter Four

1. C.H. Dodd, *According to the Scriptures* (London: Collins, 1965), pp. 11-12.

2. *Ibid.*, pp. 127-128.

3. See Dodd's thesis on this, in relation to the thesis of J. Rendel Harris, *ibid.*, pp. 26-27.

4. Dodd's modestly proposed view: It was Jesus himself, *ibid.*, pp. 109-110.

5. Hans von Campenhausen, *The Formation of the Christian Bible*, trans. by J.A. Baker (Philadelphia: Fortress Press, 1972), p. 28.

6. L. Cerfaux, *Introduction à la Bible*, ed. by A. Robert and A. Feuillet, Vol. 2 (Tournai: Desclée & Cie, 1959), pp. 406-408. There is an English translation of this volume, *Introduction to the New Testament*, by P.W. Skehan et al. (New York: Desclée, 1965).

7. For a study of Paul's use of *nous*, see Pierre Bonnard, "L'intelligence chez saint Paul," *L'Evangile, hier et aujourd'hui: Mélanges offerts au Professeur Franz-J. Leenhardt* (Geneva: Labor et Fides, 1968), pp. 13-24.

8. A. Gelin, *Introduction à la Bible* (see n. 6 supra), Vol. 1, 1957, p. 478, in his study of "Les livres prophétiques postérieurs."

9. The "authority" of Jesus is a familiar topic; see, for example, Günther Bornkamm, *Jesus of Nazareth*, trans. by I. and F. McLuskey, with J.M. Robinson (London: Hodder and Stoughton, 1960), pp. 57, 60, 97, 99 (further references in the Index).

10. See J. Giblet, "Les Promesses de l'Esprit et la Mission des Apôtres dans les Évangiles," *Irénikon* 30 (1957): 5-43.

11. Campenhausen, *op. cit.* (n. 5 supra).

12. *Ibid.*, p. 147. Campenhausen's main point is that there are at this time no normative written documents, but it seems a little exaggerated, in view of my previous section, to say that "Christians just 'know.' "

13. *Ibid.*, pp. 164-165.

14. *Ibid.*, p. 182.

15. *Ibid.*, p. 185.

16. *Ibid.*, p. 186.

17. *Ibid.*, p. 205.

18. *Ibid.*, p. 211.

19. *Ibid.*, p. 228.

20. *Ibid.*, p. 230.

21. *Ibid.*, p. 243.

22. *Ibid.*, pp. 285-286.

23. *Ireneus Against Heresies*, trans. by A. Roberts and W.H. Rambaut, *ANCL*, Vol. 5, 1868, Book 1, Preface, no. 1, p. 1.

24. *Ibid.*, Bk. 3, ch. 3, no. 3, p. 262.

25. *Ibid.*, Bk. 3, ch. 4, no. 1, p. 264.

26. *On Prescription against Heretics*, trans. by C. Dodgson, *LF*, Vol. 10, 1842, no. 19, pp. 451-452.

27. *Ibid.*, no. 20, pp. 452-453.

28. *Ibid.*, no. 21, p. 454.

29. *Ibid.*, no. 45, pp. 479-480.

30. *Epistle of S. Athanasius . . . in Defence of the Nicene Tradition*, trans. by J.H. Newman, *LF*, Vol. 8, 1842, no. 2, p. 4.

31. *Ibid.*, no. 3, p. 6.

32. *Ibid.*

33. *Ibid.*, no. 4, p. 7.

34. *Ibid.*, no. 25, p. 42.

35. *Epistle of S. Athanasius . . . concerning the Councils Held at Ariminum in Italy and at Seleucia in Isauria*, trans. by J.H. Newman, *LF*, Vol. 8, 1842, no. 5, p. 80; see nos. 3-4, pp. 76-79.

36. *Ibid.*, nos. 7, 13, 14, pp. 82, 90-91, 92.

37. *Contra epistulam Parmeniani*, Liber 3, c. 4, in Migne, *Patrologia latina*, Vol. 43, col. 101.

38. Emmanuel Amand de Mendieta, *The "Unwritten" and "Secret" APOSTOLIC TRADITIONS in the Theological Thought of St. Basil of Caesarea*, Scottish Journal of Theology Occasional Papers, No. 13 (Edinburgh: Oliver and Boyd, 1965).

39. Heiko A. Oberman, *Scottish Journal of Theology* 16 (1963): 234-236, in his article, "Quo vadis? Tradition from Ireneus to Humani Generis," pp. 225-255.

40. Vincent of Lerins, *Commonitories*, trans. by Rudolph E. Morris, in *The Fathers of the Church*, Vol. 7 (New York: 1949), ch. 2, p. 270: "In the Catholic Church itself, every care should be taken to hold fast to what has been believed everywhere, always, and by all." This phrase, "quod ubique, quod semper, quod ab omnibus" has functioned prominently as a criterion of Catholic doctrine, and therefore as a test of the *loci* adduced.

41. Saint Thomas has his own little adjustable rule for *loci*: Against the

Jews you can use the Old Testament, against heretics the New, but against Mohammedans and pagans you can use only reason, *Summa contra Gentiles*, Liber 1, c. 2.

42. For example, H.A. Oberman, *Forerunners of the Reformation. The Shape of Late Medieval Thought* (New York: Holt, Rinehart and Winston, 1966).

43. Paul De Vooght, *Les Sources de la doctrine chrétienne d'après les théologiens du XIVe siècle et du debut du XVe* . . . (Printed at Bruges for Desclée De Brouwer, 1954).

44. For a somewhat different view on Wycliffe's part in this drama, see Michael Hurley, " 'Scriptura sola': Wycliffe and his Critics," *Traditio* 16 (1960): 275-352.

45. See ch. 3, n. 17, supra.

46. Quoted by R.H. Fife, *The Revolt of Martin Luther* (New York: Columbia University Press, 1957), pp. 315-316.

47. *Ibid.*, p. 315.

48. *The Book of Concord. The Confessions of the Evangelical Lutheran Church*, trans. and ed. by T.G. Tappert et al. (Philadelphia: Fortress Press, 1959).

49. Denzinger-Schönmetzer (see ch. 3, no. 20, supra), no. 1501: "in libris scriptis et sine scripto traditionibus." J.R. Geiselmann has written extensively on the "partim . . . partim" question; see, for example, "Un malentendu éclairci: La relation 'Écriture-Tradition' dans la théologie catholique," *Istina* 5 (1958): 197-214; but see also Joseph Ratzinger, "On the Interpretation of the Tridentine Decree on Tradition," in Karl Rahner & Joseph Ratzinger, *Revelation and Tradition*, Quaestiones Disputatae, 17, trans. by W.J. O'Hara (Montreal: Palm Publishers, 1966), pp. 50-68.

50. *Melchioris Cani . . . Opera theologica*, 3 vols. (Rome: Forzani et soc., 1898, 1899, 1900). The *De locis theologicis* extends through the first 2 vols. and much of the 3rd.

Chapter Five

1. E.C. Blackman, "See," *TWBB*, p. 223. Also, C. Traets, *Voir Jésus et le Père en lui selon l'Evangile de saint Jean* (Rome: Gregorian University Press, 1967).

2. James M. Robinson, *The Problem of History in Mark*, Studies in Biblical Theology, No. 21 (London: SCM, 1957), p. 76. Robinson's reference is specifically to two things in Mark "which are not 'understood': the feedings (6.52; 8.17, 21) and the parables (4.12; 7.14). In neither of these cases is it really a matter of comprehending intellectually a doctrine."

3. Pierre Grelot, *Introduction à la Bible* (see ch. 4, n. 6, supra), Vol. 1, 1957, pp. 173-178, in his study, "L'interprétation catholique des livres saints."

4. C.H. Dodd, *According to the Scriptures* (London: Collins, 1965), pp. 127-128. "But instances . . . are rare," Dodd adds.

5. Robert M. Grant, *The Interpreter's Bible*, Vol. 1 (New York: Abingdon, 1952), in his article "History of the Interpretation of the Bible (Ancient Period)," pp. 106-114. Grant finds two occurrences of allegorical

method in the scriptures: "The first and most famous instance is found in Gal. 4:21-24. . . . The other example is in the Revelation of John. . . . In a description of the fall of . . . Jerusalem, the author explains that allegorically it is called Sodom and Egypt, for the Lord was crucified there" (p. 107).

6. Among the many guides we have on this question, I may refer to Sir Edwyn Hoskyns and Noel Davey, *The Riddle of the New Testament* (London: Faber and Faber, 1958); see their ch. 5.

7. Norman Perrin, *What Is Redaction Criticism?* (Philadelphia: Fortress Press, 1969).

8. *ODCC*, p. 514, in the article, "Form-Criticism." Emphasis as in the original.

9. E. Basil Redlich, *Form Criticism: Its Value and Limitations* (London: Duckworth, 1956; reprinted from 1939 original), p. 55. Redlich does not agree with this assumption of form-criticism; his own formulation would be: "The vital factors which preserved the tradition are to be found in the practical interests of the Christian community" (p. 62).

10. *Ibid.*, p. 56; Redlich is still presenting an assumption, that of Dibelius.

11. In the following three paragraphs I am indebted chiefly to Robert M. Grant, *op. cit.* (n. 5 supra), and to K. Grobel, "Interpretation, History and Principles of," *IDB*, Vol. 2, 1962, pp. 718-24. I have used Grant for the early period up to Augustine and Jerome, and Grobel for the subsequent period up to Luther.

12. Grant, *op. cit.* (n. 5 supra), p. 107. A slot for the apologists of the second century can probably be found here, so far as they pertain to the history of the word, but really they are marginal to that history: "Except for Tertullian, they were not primarily theologians. Their method was to exhibit Christianity to emperors and to the public as politically harmless and morally and culturally superior to paganism," *ODCC*, p. 71.

13. But there was a real beginning at this time in the formulation of scientific methods of exegesis; Bernard Lonergan refers to "the crisp principles of Clement of Alexandria" in contrast to "the struggles of Ireneus" (*Method*, 296, n. 2).

14. Grant, *op. cit.* (n. 5 supra), p. 111.

15. *Ibid.*, pp. 111-113.

16. Grobel, *op. cit.* (n. 11 supra), p. 721, gives the Latin original as follows: "Littera gesta docet, quid credas allegoria, moralis quid agas, quo tendas anagogia."

17. Quoted from Luther's *Table Talk* by Grobel, *ibid.*, p. 723.

18. E.C. Blackman, "The Task of Exegesis," *The Background of the New Testament and Its Eschatology*, ed. by W.D. Davies and D. Daube in Honour of Charles Harold Dodd (Cambridge at the University Press, 1956), pp. 3-26. See also his *Biblical Interpretation* (London: Independent Press, 1957), ch. 5. Blackman is adamant, however, on literal exegesis as the first task.

19. S. Schmidt, "De Protestantium exegesi 'pneumatica'," *Verbum Domini* 25 (1947): 12-22, 65-73.

20. The authority on the *sensus plenior* is Raymond E. Brown; see his book, *The* Sensus Plenior *of Sacred Scripture* (Baltimore: St. Mary's University, 1955); for subsequent interest in the idea, see his article "The Sen-

sus Plenior in the Last Ten Years," *The Catholic Biblical Quarterly* 25 (1963): 262-285, but for its later rapid decline, see his further study, "The Problems of the *Sensus Plenior,*" *Ephemerides theologicae lovanienses* 43 (1967): 460-469.

21. I do not myself repudiate the *sensus plenior*, but I do not think it serves a useful purpose; further, it tends to coincidence with the meaning of history to be discussed in chapter six—the full divine meaning of God's written word is the divine plan manifested in his Son and creation, which is also the meaning of history.

22. Brown, *The* Sensus Plenior *of Sacred Scripture* (n. 20 supra), pp. 22-27, gives an account of the "consequent" sense.

23. See notes 31-33 infra.

24. *On First Principles* (see ch. 3, n. 25, supra), Bk. 1, Preface, nos. 3-4, pp. 2-3.

25. *Epistle . . . in Defence of the Nicene Tradition* (see ch. 4, n. 30, supra), no. 20, p. 35; see also nos. 19, 30-32.

26. *De civitate Dei*, Liber 16, c. 2, 1, in *Patrologia latina*, Vol. 41, col. 477: "Multa . . . dum haereticorum calida inquietudine exagitantur . . . et considerantur diligentius, et intelliguntur clarius, et instantius praedicantur: et ab adversario mota quaestio, discendi existit occasio."

27. Vincent of Lerins, *op. cit.* (see ch. 4, n. 40, supra), ch. 23, p. 309. This translation weakens considerably Vincent's "in eodem . . . dogmate, eodem sensu, eademque sententia." Other texts may be found in J.H. Walgrave, *Unfolding Revelation: The Nature of Doctrinal Development* (Philadelphia: Westminster Press, 1972), ch. 4, though it seems to me Walgrave inflates their meaning a little to find evidence of views on development.

28. Owen Chadwick, *From Bossuet to Newman: The Idea of Doctrinal Development* (Cambridge at the University Press, 1957).

29. On the early history of the Catholic faculty of theology at Tübingen, see Mark Schoof, *A Survey of Catholic Theology 1800-1970*, trans. by N.D. Smith (Glen Rock, N.J.: Paulist Newman Press, 1970), pp. 22-30. That Newman had not read Möhler is clear from the way the latter is referred to in the *Essay*; see John Henry Cardinal Newman, *An Essay on the Development of Christian Doctrine*, Foreword by Gustave Weigel (Garden City, N.Y.: Doubleday Image Book, 1960), p. 53 (in Newman's Introduction, no. 21).

30. J.H. Newman, *Fifteen Sermons Preached Before the University of Oxford*, 3rd ed. (London: Longmans, Green & Co., 1918), sermon 15, The Theory of Developments in Religious Doctrine.

31. Newman, *An Essay . . . op. cit.* (see n. 29, supra), pp. 34, 36 (nos. 4, 7, in Newman's Introduction).

32. *Ibid.*, pp. 59-60 (ch. 1, section 1, nos. 4-5).

33. *Ibid.*, p. 63 (no. 7).

34. Gustave Weigel, "Foreword," *ibid.*, p. 12.

35. *Ibid.*, chs. 7 to 12; in ch. 5 Newman had set up the seven elements in theory.

36. Fr. M.M. Tuyaerts, *L'Évolution du Dogme, Étude théologique* (Louvain: "Nova et Vetera," 1919). For a perspective on the work of Tuyaerts, I am indebted to Henri de Lubac, *Recherches de science religieuse* 35 (1948): passim, in his "Bulletin de théologie fondamentale. Le

problème du développement du dogme," pp. 130-160.

37. L. Charlier, *Essai sur le problème théologique* (Thuillies, 1938). There is a long exposition and critique of this book by T. Zapelena, "Problema theologicum," *Gregorianum* 24 (1943): 23-47, 287-326; 25 (1944): 38-73. Charlier's book is itself out of circulation.

38. *The Rediscovery of Newman: An Oxford Symposium*, ed. by J. Coulson and A.M. Allchin (London: Sheed and Ward, 1967); see p. vii.

39. See Nicholas Lash, *Change in Focus: A study of doctrinal change and continuity* (London: Sheed and Ward, 1973), who is of this opinion too. Lash's book came to my attention after I had written chapter five, but I do not believe his work will require any radical revision in mine.

40. Modernism is a campaign on many fronts. Lash sees it in the perspective of development; I see it in the slightly different perspective of the history of the theology of the word.

41. This insight into Paul's tactics (or are they Luke's?) is not my own but I have lost the reference to my source.

42. Daniel D. Williams, *A Handbook of Christian Theology* (Cleveland: World Publishing Co., 1958), p. 233, in the article "Modernism."

43. Alec R. Vidler, *20th Century Defenders of the Faith* (New York: Seabury Press, 1965), p. 40.

44. *Ibid.*, p. 49, quoting G. Tyrrell's *Christianity at the Cross Roads*, 1963, p. 95.

45. Vidler, *op. cit.*, pp. 42-43, quoting *L'Évangile et l'Église*, 5th French ed. (Paris, 1929), pp. 153f.

46. Vidler, *op. cit.*, p. 43, again quoting *L'Évangile . . .*, p. 166.

47. I mean a need in the world of objective discourse; what personal need the *Essay* may have met for Newman himself is another question.

48. Lash, *op. cit.*, (n. 39 supra), p. 136, gives Schillebeeckx credit for pointing out "that the problems studied in catholic theology under the rubric of 'doctrinal development' are, fundamentally, the same problems which, in recent decades, protestant theology has preferred to discuss in terms of 'hermeneutics.' " I cannot now remember when I first noticed this similarity, but it may well have been suggested to me by reading Schillebeeckx; if so, I am happy to acknowledge the debt.

49. "Christ has two natures. And what is that to me? If he bears the magnificent and consoling name of Christ, it is because of the ministry and the task he took upon himself; it is that which gives him his name." This much-quoted text is given in French translation by Yves Congar, *Le Christ, Marie, et l'Église* (Bruges: Desclée De Brouwer, 1952), p. 33; I have lost the source of my English translation. Another famous text is that of Melanchthon: "Hoc est Christum cognoscere, beneficia ejus cognoscere." But J.S. Whale, *The Protestant Tradition: An Essay in Interpretation* (Cambridge at the University Press, 1962), p. 331, informs us that Melanchthon withdrew it from later editions of his *Loci communes*. Paul Ricoeur remarks that the "application" of traditional hermeneutic has become the "appropriation" of modern thinking, *Studies in Religion* 5 (1975-1976) 29, in his article, "Philosophical hermeneutics and theological hermeneutics," pp. 14-33.

50. S. Kierkegaard, *Training in Christianity . . .*, trans. by Walter Lowrie (Princeton University Press, 1944), passim; Lowrie's Index, *s.v.* "Contemporaneous," gives only a fraction of the references. See also Kier-

kegaard's *Philosophical Fragments* . . . , trans. by David F. Swenson (Princeton: Princeton University Press, 1936), ch. 4 (The Case of the Contemporary Disciple), Interlude, and ch. 5 (The Disciple at Second Hand).

51. *Kierkegaard's Attack Upon "Christendom" 1854-1855*, trans. by Walter Lowrie (Princeton: Princeton University Press, 1944), p. 120.

52. Wm. Hordern, *New Directions in Theology Today*, Vol. 1: *Introduction* (Philadelphia: Westminster Press, 1966), p. 25.

53. R. Bultmann, "Bultmann Replies to His Critics," in *Kerygma and Myth*, ed. by H.W. Bartsch (New York: Harper Torchbook, 1961), pp. 191-211; see p. 192.

54. Hordern, *op. cit.* (n. 52 supra), pp. 42-43. His example is music, which "can be understood only by someone who already knows something about music."

55. Bultmann, *op. cit.* (n. 53 supra), p. 192.

56. Hordern, *op. cit.* (n. 52 supra), p. 59.

57. James M. Robinson, "Hermeneutic Since Barth," in *The New Hermeneutic*, New Frontiers in Theology, ed. by James M. Robinson and John B. Cobb, Jr., Vol. 2 (New York: Harper & Row, 1964), 1-77; see pp. 52, 68, and passim.

58. *Ibid.*, p. 38.

59. *Ibid.*, p. 50.

60. *Ibid.*, p. 48.

61. *Ibid.*, p. 46.

62. *Ibid.*, p. 48.

63. Helmut Franz: "The basic thing about a text is not what the author intended to express in words by following up a given point of view. Rather, basic is what wills fundamentally to show itself and have its say prior to or apart from any subjective intent. The question to the text would then not be the question as to the [author's] perspective, but rather: 'What shines forth in this text? What shows itself in this text?' " quoted by Robinson, *ibid.*, p. 46.

64. Robinson, *ibid.*, p. 57.

65. *Ibid.*, p. 61.

66. *Ibid.*

67. *Ibid.*, pp. 62-63.

68. *Ibid.*, p. 4.

69. Quoted by Robinson, *ibid.*, p. 67.

70. *Ibid.*, p. 68.

71. Quoted by Robinson, *ibid.*, p. 63.

Chapter Six

1. Owen Chadwick, *From Bossuet to Newman: The Idea of Doctrinal Development* (Cambridge at the University Press, 1957), p. 195.

2. On this question I have been helped by the work of Werner Bulst, *Revelation* (New York: Sheed and Ward, 1965). See also for the New Testament, Wolfhart Pannenberg, "The Revelation of God in Jesus of Nazareth," in *Theology as History*, New Frontiers in Theology, ed. by James M. Robinson and John B. Cobb, Jr., Vol. 3 (New York: Harper & Row, 1967), pp. 101-133.

3. See *Essays on Typology*, ed. by G.W.H. Lampe and K.J. Wooll-Combe (London: SCM, 57), especially Woollcombe's article "The Biblical Origins and Patristic Development of Typology," pp. 39-75. He is at pains to distinguish allegory, typology, and fulfillment of prophecy, and finds a great theological difference between Paul and Philo; in the latter it is almost impossible to separate typology from allegorism (p. 65).

4. Jean Daniélou, *From Shadows to Reality. Studies in the Biblical Typology of the Fathers*, translation by W. Hibberd of *Sacramentum futuri* . . . (London: Burns & Oates, 1960).

5. *Ibid.*, p. 61: "Allegory is not a sense of Scripture at all." P. 64: "It would be an entire abuse of language to include moral allegory with typology under the one heading of the spiritual sense, as opposed to the literal sense: typology is a legitimate extension of the literal sense, while moral allegory is something entirely alien: the former is in truth exegesis, the latter is not." P. 288: In typology "we are face to face with something which is part and parcel of the deposit of Revelation."

6. R.M. Grant, *A Short History of the Interpretation of the Bible*, rev. ed. (New York: Macmillan, 1963), pp. 99-101.

7. The obvious place to look in St. Thomas is the *Summa theologiae*, where the idea is set forth in Part 1, q. 1, a. 10. But the fullest treatment occurs in *Quodlibet VII*, q. 6, aa. 1-3. See also Thomas's scriptural commentary on Paul's allegory in Galatians.

8. Bernard J.F. Lonergan, *Grace and Freedom: Operative Grace in the Thought of St. Thomas Aquinas*, ed. by J. Patout Burns (London: Darton, Longman & Todd, 1971), p. 63.

9. Jean Pierre de Caussade, *Abandonment to Divine Providence*, 3rd English ed. from the French ed. of J. Ramière (St. Louis: B. Herder Book Co., n.d.; Introduction by Dom Arnold 1921), p. 15.

10. *Ibid.*, p. 29.

11. *Ibid.*, p. 24.

12. *Ibid.*, pp. 20-21.

13. *Ibid.*, p. 23.

14. *Ibid.*, p. 28.

15. *Ibid.*, pp. 21-22.

16. *Ibid.*, p. 21.

17. *Ibid.*, p. 22.

18. *Ibid.*, p. 15.

19. The influence of Ignatius of Loyola (seeing God in all things) on de Caussade is one example of such a thread through history.

20. Most of the following paragraph relies on the article "History," in *Sacramentum mundi*, Vol. 3 (Montreal: Palm Publishers, 1969), pp. 31-47, which has sections by Darlap, Splett, Hünermann, and Kasper. See also P. Hug, "History, Theology of," *New Catholic Encyclopedia*, Vol. 7 (New York: McGraw-Hill, 1967), pp. 26-31.

21. Wolfhart Pannenberg, "Hermeneutics and Universal History," *Journal for Theology and the Church*, Vol. 4 (History and Hermeneutic), 1967, pp. 122-152.

22. *Ibid.*, p. 123.

23. *Ibid.*, p. 132.

24. *Ibid.*

25. *Ibid.*

26. *Ibid.*, p. 133.
27. *Ibid.*, p. 134.
28. *Ibid.*, p. 137.
29. *Ibid.*, p. 138.
30. *Ibid.*, p. 139.
31. *Ibid.*, p. 140.
32. *Ibid.*, p. 141.
33. *Ibid.*, pp. 141-142.
34. *Ibid.*, pp. 142-144.
35. *Ibid.*, p. 146.
36. *Ibid.*
37. *Ibid.*
38. *Ibid.*, p. 141.
39. *Ibid.*, p. 151.
40. *Ibid.*
41. *Revelation as History*, ed. by Wolfhart Pannenberg et ʹal. (New York: Macmillan, 1968). See Pannenberg's own article, "Dogmatic Theses on the Doctrine of Revelation," pp. 123-158.
42. *Ibid.*, p. 125.
43. *Ibid.*, p. 131.
44. *Ibid.*, p. 139.
45. *Ibid.*, p. 145.
46. *Ibid.*, p. 152.
47. See his Thesis 7, just quoted, explained *ibid.*, pp. 152-155.
48. See Otto Weber, *Karl Barth's Church Dogmatics* . . ., trans. by A.C. Cochrane (Philadelphia: Westminster Press, 1953), pp. 23-27. Dietrich Ritschl, *A Theology of Proclamation* (Richmond: Knox Press, 1960), pp. 28-29, 42-43, concedes that the revealed Word is first in authority, but prefers the reverse order, that of hearing the word, in which the preached word is first.
49. Quoted by René Marlé, *Introduction to Hermeneutics*, trans. by E. Froment and R. Albrecht (New York: Herder and Herder, 1967), pp. 27-28.
50. It seems to be the fear of Gerhard Ebeling, *The Problem of Historicity in the Church and Its Proclamation*, trans. by G. Foley (Philadelphia: Fortress Press, 1967), pp. 72-80, that history as revelation involves a dualism; it turns this revelation into an objective event that must then in a second moment be subjectively appropriated. See also Dale Stover, p. 41 of his article "Linguisticality and theology: Applying the hermeneutics of Hans-Georg Gadamer," *Studies in Religion* 5 (1975-1976): 34-44.

Chapter Seven

1. We touch here on the miserable subject/object question, on which the reader has a right to ask my views, though I confess to a great impatience with much of the discussion. My position is simple: There are subjects, there are objects, there is a valid distinction between them, and a valid question on their relationship, which question can be put from different viewpoints, those, for example, of phenomenology, of epistemology, of ontology. Two things foul up the discussion: (1) the baseless supposition

that we first know subjects and then have a problem reaching knowledge of objects, and (2) the supposed indignity subjects suffer in being "reduced" to the status of objects. As to the first, what we know is the things that are, and among them we come to distinguish subjects and objects (with objects having the priority in the implicit objectivity of all knowledge). As to the second, there is communion of subjects and there is discourse, and it is just nonsense to forbid the second on the ground of the excellence of the first. To pray "O God, my Lord" does not invalidate my explanation in a theology lecture of the Lordship of God.

2. Jean Lévêque, "Intériorité.—I. Le thème dans la Bible," *Dictionnaire de Spiritualité, Ascétique et Mystique*, Vol. 7² (Paris: Beauchesne, 1971), cols. 1877-1889.

3. *Ibid.*, col. 1886.

4. *Ibid.*, col. 1887.

5. If the question "What are we to do?" is considered merely as an investigation in ethics, it reverts to a question for intelligence. But in the present context it clearly refers to an exercise of personal responsibility; it is a question for deliberation.

6. For somewhat more detail on the first two levels of questioning, see my article, "Neither Jew nor Greek, but One Human Nature and Operation in All," *Philippine Studies* 13 (1965): 546-571.

7. Gerhard Friedrich, "Prophêtes," *TDNT*, Vol. 6, 1968, pp. 842-843.

8. *Ibid.*, p. 847.

9. G. Rovea, "Interiorità," *Enciclopedia Filosofica*, Vol. 2 (Venice/Rome: Istituto per la Collaborazione Culturale, 1957), col. 1480.

10. *Ibid.*, col. 1481.

11. See Rovea (*ibid.*) for references for the quotations from Augustine; he gives as the source of the last quotation in my paragraph, M.F. Sciacca, *S. Agostino*, I, (Brescia, 1950), p. 132.

12. Bernard Lonergan, "Subject and Soul," *Philippine Studies* 13 (1965): 576-585. Substantially the same article appears as Introduction in David Burrell's edition of *Verbum: Word and Idea in Aquinas* (University of Notre Dame Press, 1967; First published in *Theological Studies*, 1946-1949), pp. vii-xv. I shall refer to the latter (except for one passage not reproduced there), but the reader should not fail to note the significant title of the *Philippine Studies* article.

13. *Verbum*, p. viii.

14. *Ibid.*, p. x.

15. *Ibid.*, p. ix.

16. *Ibid.*, p. xiii.

17. *Ibid.*, p. ix.

18. "Subject and Soul," *loc cit.*, p. 576. This passage is not included in *Verbum*.

19. A different perspective governs the work of Roberto Busa, *La Terminologia Tomistica dell'Interiorità*, Archivum Philosophicum Aloisianum, Serie II, 4 (Milan: Fratelli Bocca, 1949); the approach is metaphysical, and the main interest lies in the manner of God's presence in his creatures.

20. *Summa theologiae*, 1-2, q. 49, prologus.

21. *Ibid.*, q. 90, prologus.

22. *Ibid.*, q. 106, a. 1 c.

23. B. Lonergan, *Verbum* (n. 12 supra), pp. 80-81; the Thomist quotation is from *De veritate,* q. 10, a. 6 c.

24. See pp. 125-127 in my article "Universal Norms and the Concrete 'Operabile' in St. Thomas Aquinas," *Sciences ecclésiastiques* 7 (1955): 115-149.

25. The classical exposition of consciousness as inner experience is B. Lonergan's *De constitutione Christi ontologica et psychologica* (Rome: Gregorian University Press, 1956); see especially Part 5, De conscientia humana, pp. 83-99, and passim in Part 6. Unfortunately, this work is not yet available in English, but the reader may consult Lonergan's *Collection* (New York: Herder and Herder, 1969), pp. 175-187, and *Insight* (London: Longmans, Green and Co., 1957), pp. 320-321.

26. See the chapter titles of *The Following of Christ*, for example, Book 2, ch. 1: Of Interior Conversation; Book 3, ch. 1: Of the Internal Discourse of Christ to a Faithful Soul; etc. The dictum on feeling compunction is in Book 1, ch. 1.

27. See Cornelio Fabro, "Esperienza religiosa," *Enciclopedia Cattolica*, Vol. 5 (Città del Vaticano, 1950), cols. 601-607, for a sketchy history. There is a helpful study of a collateral movement in Colin Morris, *The Discovery of the Individual 1050-1200*, Church History Outlines, 5 (London: S.P.C.K., 1972).

28. *Summa theologiae*, 1, q. 1, a. 6 ad 3m. The topic is often studied by the Thomists under the heading of connaturality.

29. H. Pinard, "Expérience religieuse," in *Dictionnaire de Théologie Catholique*, Vol. 5^2 (Paris: Letouzey, 1939), cols. 1786-1868; the quotation from Pascal is in col. 1795.

30. *Ibid.*, col. 1799.

31. *Ibid.*, col. 1801.

32. *Kierkegaard's Concluding Unscientific Postscript*, trans. by David F. Swenson and Walter Lowrie (Princeton: Princeton University Press, 1944), p. 182; see the Index for other passages on "Inwardness." H. Bouillard, *Karl Barth*, Vol. 1 (Paris: Aubier, 1957), pp. 110-111, informs us that Barth rejected Kierkegaard's interiority.

33. See the Index of *Insight* (n. 25 supra) *s.v.* "Experience-Understanding-Reflection," and that of *Method* (see Introduction, n. 3 supra) *s.v.* "Levels of conscious intentionality."

34. See *Verbum* (n. 12 supra), ch. 2, and the Index *s.v.* "Critical."

35. See the Index of *Method s.v.* "Idealism" (or that of *Insight s.v.* "Hegel," "Husserl," "Kant," etc.).

36. The detailed study of the influences Lonergan's thought underwent has been badly neglected; of course, they are extremely difficult to trace.

37. *Theology of Renewal.* Vol. 1: *Renewal of Religious Thought*, ed. by L.K. Shook (Montreal: Palm Publishers, 1968), pp. 34-46. Lonergan's contribution was reprinted in *A Second Collection*, ed. by W.F.J. Ryan and B.J. Tyrrell (London: Darton, Longman & Todd, 1974), pp. 55-67.

38. *A Second Collection*, p. 67.

39. For the next several paragraphs references to *Method* will be given in the text.

40. Lonergan's use of "inner" and "outer" word here should not be confused with the same verbal usage in *Verbum* (see the Index to that work *s.v.* "Word"). The inner word of *Verbum* is the concept expressing in-

teriorly an act of understanding; it is poles apart from the inner word of *Method*; on the other hand, the outer word of one work is closely related to that of the other.

Conclusion and Projections

1. *A Second Collection* (see ch. 7, n. 37 supra), p. 161, in "The Future of Christianity."

Appendix

1. Chrysostome Larcher, in the symposium *La Parole de Dieu en Jésus-Christ* (Tournai: Casterman, 1961), p. 59; Larcher's contribution is entitled "La Parole de Dieu en tant que Révélation dans l'Ancien Testament," pp. 35-67.